LAL BAHADUR SHASTRI

Lessons in Leadership

2nd October 1904 – 11th January 1966

LAL BAHADUR SHASTRI

Lessons in Leadership

Anil Shastri - Pavan Choudary

Wisdom Village Publications Pvt Ltd
Knowledge is information. Wisdom is transformation.

A WISDOM VILLAGE PRESENTATION

Books from Wisdom Village Publications envision to enhance and enrich their readers with life changing experiences from the business, mind, body and soul genres. They strive towards holistic development.

Editorial Coordinator Anu Anand

ISBN 9789380710365

Published in 2014 by:

Wisdom Village Publications Pvt Ltd
Knowledge is information. Wisdom is transformation.

www.wisdomvillagepublications.com

To Book Your Orders:
Email: wvpdindia@gmail.com
Or Call: +91 9810800469

Published by Anu Anand;
Cover Design and Page Setting by Sunil Mathur;
Illustrations by Rajani Mathur;

Printed in India by Manipal Technologies Limited, Manipal

Acknowledgments

We would like to thank:

Anu Anand, Publisher, for the extensive research and numerous meetings she took with us in putting the insights from Shastriji's life and the lessons that we could draw. She made the task of knitting the book take a fraction of the time it would have taken authors like us who have a day job.

Anamika Vishwanathan for stringing our thoughts together into a well thought out structure and for editing the book.

Sunil and Rajani Mathur for making the book come alive with creative illustrations.

Manju Shastri for the many insights she provided, the critics she offered and the warmth which she spreads.

Our families for letting us have the many evenings which we spent on the book.

And to Manisha for typing the anecdotes and coordinating with the publisher.

Index

Introduction

This book is about a man who came from the humblest section of society and rose to the highest position of the land. He was the epitome of wisdom and practicality. The values he lived by have transcended time and generations and have proved to be invaluable not only today but will continue to be so in the future. As you go through this book, you will find several recollections and anecdotes from Shastri's childhood, his public office and adult life. Unfortunately, he was snatched away by the cruel jaws of death early. However, the principles he lived by endure.

I have hand-picked personal recollections of his second son Anil Shastri who had the good fortune of being raised by such a stalwart. During my interactions with Anil, I saw in him the same integrity, honesty and loyalty his father was known for. I saw that despite his time in politics and presiding over an educational empire his value system was uncontaminated. And that beneath his dignified exterior he is a simple, unpretentious and affable man. And there was always this glint of pride in his eyes while reminiscing times spent with his father. Only a great father would inspire such pride. I could see the same emotion resonating from other people who had interacted with Lal Bahadur in his lifetime. Little wonder then that Lal Bahadur Shastri was the first person to be awarded Bharat Ratna posthumously, the highest civilian honour in the country, in 1966. He was a true jewel of the country.

What struck me the most about Lal Bahadur Shastri was that despite coming from a very humble background, he rose to high ranks through his hard work and wisdom. Poverty did not vanquish him, rather it propelled him to reach the highest position the country offered. Besides, he did not lose his empathy for others. He felt the pain of others when he put himself in their place. This was evident in the way he dealt with people from all walks of life. His profound empathy, however, did not take away from acting fair and just. Nothing confounded him and he was known to take quick and decisive decisions whether it pertained to war with Pakistan or action in Kashmir.

Shastri was also noted for his good habits of punctuality, practicality and hospitality. No one would ever go back hurt or disappointed after meeting him. He made everyone feel welcome and positive, even though, at times, the way forward may not have been entirely favourable for them. He also did not believe in hierarchy which in-subordinated people. He was inclusive and discussed issues with everyone, drawing nuggets from all levels.

Being a man of few needs, Lal Bahadur believed in living within means and cutting the coat according to the cloth. Whenever he had some spare resources, he would plough these back into the community to help the needy. He did not believe in ostentation but proudly flaunted his Indianness. I believe that today's generation can learn a lot from this iconic personality.

Drawing from such a wellspring of rich values, this book is presented in three sections – Values to inspire us at an **individual level**, **interpersonal level** and **societal level.** Each of these recollections has a thought-provoking and inspiring lesson which if applied, can help us develop into well-rounded personalities.

Pavan Choudary

Values to Inspire us at an Individual Level

"Your beliefs become your thoughts,
Your thoughts become your words,
Your words become your actions,
Your actions become your habits,
Your habits become your character,
Your character becomes your destiny."

- Mahatma Gandhi

Lal Bahadur Shastri was a man of impeccable values and principles. He stood by them firmly right through his life. Even in testing times, he did not flinch or compromise. Whether it was living within meagre means, not expecting or giving preferential treatment, being fair to everyone and fulfilling his duties as a family man and father, he was an exemplary beacon.

This section focuses on Shastriji's personal values which made him a leader for all ages.

Gardener's Advice

(Circa 1910)

When Lal Bahadur Shastri was about six years old, he once visited an orchard with his friends. While his friends climbed the trees, he decided to stay on the ground. Shastriji was fond of flowers from the beginning and plucked a rose from one of the flower beds. The gardener of the orchard assumed that Shastriji was stealing his flowers so he went up to him and scolded him harshly which made Shastriji weep. He said, "Don't scold me as my father died when I was only ½ years old."

The gardener sympathized with him but told him straight, "All the more reason that you must exhibit better behaviour my boy, and not take anything in future without the owner's permission." These words impacted Shastriji and he assured the gardener that he would be very careful in future. When he became the Prime Minister he remembered to meet him during his next visit to Varanasi. He thanked the gardener for his piece of advice.

Wisdom Window

The gardener's words pierced Shastri's conscience. He realized that he could not expect to have his parents' support to push him forward in life. He would have to manage moving up the echelons himself with the help of right conduct.

Lal Bahadur also learnt that when you live with good values, brick by brick, you construct a temple through your good conduct. By the time it is ready, you realize, it is also a castle. It has made you impregnable. The robe has become the armour.

There is also a strong lesson here for less privileged people (less privileged in looks, financial condition or family support, etc). They need to conduct themselves extraordinarily to be respected in the society.

Toiling at School

(Circa 1912)

While at school, Lal Bahadur was too poor to afford books. Once the whole class was asked to bring their English Reader book with them the next day by their English teacher. The teacher also asked the students to prepare two chapters for the class as he would ask questions the following day. Since Shastri was too poor to afford books, he did not own books but borrowed them from friends to prepare for lessons. On this occasion too, he asked one of his friends to lend the English Reader to him for a few hours. Initially the friend hesitated but then knowing the plight of his little friend, lent his book for a few hours.

Lal Bahadur Shastri assiduously copied the entire English Reader and returned the book to his friend. He then prepared the two chapters the whole night and was ready with his answers the next day. The class teacher though impressed by his answers, was annoyed with Lal Bahadur for not having carried his English Reader to school. Before the

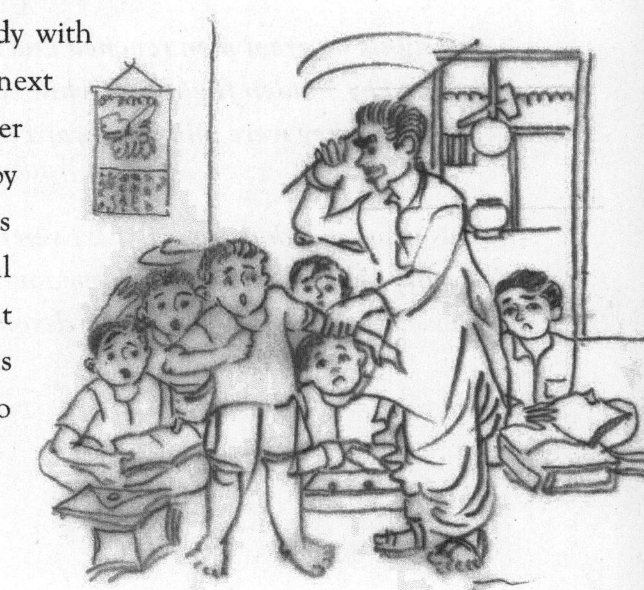

little boy could say anything, the teacher caned him. Shastriji did not utter a word.

It was only when his friends told the teacher that Lal Bahadur was from a very poor family and could not afford his school books that the class teacher was very upset with himself. He apologized to Lal Bahadur and took him to his house. From that day, the class teacher treated him like his son.

Wisdom Window

Heights by great men reached and kept were not obtained by sudden flight but, while their companions slept, they were toiling upward in the night.

- Henry Wadsworth Longfellow

This is an anecdote from 1912. Even a hundred years later, the secret of success still remains the same – doing whatever it takes to deliver results despite the deprivations you face.

Mango Vendor

(Circa 1916)

One day Lal Bahadur Shastri and his maternal uncle Lallan mama went for a stroll in Mirzapur. They saw an old man with a basket passing by. Lal Bahadur asked the old man what he had in his basket. The old man said he had mangoes. He further said, "Since it is evening now and I am going home, why don't you buy some of these luscious mangoes. You can buy 100 mangoes for just one anna which is half the rate at what I have been selling." (One anna was then one-sixteenth of a rupee. It comprised four paisas).

Lal Bahadur and Lallan mama gave 2 paisas each to the old man, who started counting the mangoes. When he reached 50, Lal Bahadur stopped him and said not to take out more. The old man was puzzled and said, "My boy, you've given me an anna and I have to give you another fifty mangoes to make up the hundred." Shastriji replied, "The money is yours. Actually we don't need more than fifty mangoes. Thank you very much." The old man looked at Lal Bahadur in disbelief, put the basket with the remaining mangoes on his head, and slowly walked away. When the old man was gone, Lallan mama said to Shastriji, "That was very foolish of you. We paid for a hundred mangoes but you've taken only fifty."

Shastriji explained to him, "You recall the old man saying he was prepared to sell a hundred mangoes for just one anna? It was a distress sale. Why take advantage of such a situation? In any case, we don't really need more than fifty mangoes for the family."

Wisdom Window

Shastri was a forerunner in fairplay. Very often people bargain hard, especially with those who can be exploited. Shastri could never condone exploiting the helpless. Moreover he was against hoarding - hoarding things just because they were coming cheap.

Vegetarianism

(Circa 1916)

Lal Bahadur Shastri's maternal uncle, Bindeshwari Prasad, was very fond of good food. He used to rear a number of birds in his Moghalsarai house and whenever he wanted to have non-vegetarian food, he would select a bird and have it cooked for dinner. One day a pigeon flew and sat on his terrace. Uncle asked Shastri to catch the pigeon and bring it down. Lal Bahadur did not get up as he knew that his uncle would kill the pigeon and eat it. Lal Bahadur was a strict vegetarian and did not want the pigeon to be killed.

When Bindeshwari Prasad realized that Lal Bahadur would not bring back the pigeon to him, he assured the little boy that he won't kill it. Only on this assurance did Lal Bahadur catch the pigeon and bring it down. But his uncle did not

keep his word and got the pigeon cooked. Lal Bahadur was appalled but helpless. He was deeply hurt and went on a hunger strike and did not eat any food all day despite persuasion by his mother and other family members. Since Lal Bahadur was much loved by the family members, all ladies in the family joined him in his brave protest and refused to eat too. The next day when the uncle found himself alone, facing the combined protest of all the family members, he promised Lal Bahadur that he wouldn't kill birds anymore and would give up non-vegetarian food. Lal Bahadur broke his fast and his uncle kept his word and became a vegetarian for the rest of his life.

This was Lal Bahadur Shastri's first exercise in satyagraha.

Wisdom Window

Lal Bahadur did not just convert his uncle to vegetarianism, he made him realize the importance of keeping his word. He did not like the fact that his uncle said one thing but did quite the other. He took a lonely stand against his uncle and was quickly joined by the ladies of the house who came to his support.

The leader has often to serve as the nucleus around which the movement later forms. This requires courage of conviction. In the beginning he stands alone, slowly a tide of humanity joins him.

'No' to Borrowing Money

(Circa 1940)

My mother Lalita Shastri once told me about an incident that took place much before I was born. In August, 1940 when my elder sister, Kusum was six years old, a mela (exhibition) was being held in town. She expressed her desire to Shastriji to visit the mela. Shastriji told her that he had no money with him for the exhibition so my mother borrowed Rs. 25/- from one of her friends and went to see the exhibition along with Shastriji and Kusum. They went from stall to stall and from one end to the other end of the exhibition but Shastriji did not allow my mother to buy anything, not even for my sister Kusum. My mother felt very bad about it.

Lalita Shastri looked visibly upset when she returned home. Shastriji said, "I know that you are angry because nothing has been purchased for you from the exhibition. It was deliberately done because you

had borrowed money from one of your friends. It looks very odd that we should buy something with the borrowed money. You should hereafter keep in mind that unless it is absolutely necessary to purchase a thing we should not borrow money."

Since then my mother made it a point never to borrow money from anyone for anything, urgent or otherwise.

Wisdom Window

Borrowing was a taboo in Shastri's time as the credit system had not fully evolved then. The money lenders were extremely exploitative and many a time, usurped the collaterals provided by the borrowers.

Shastri believed that one should borrow only to invest in assured return investments like property, house, education or factory, and not for catching up with the Jones'.

Today, the credit market has evolved and borrowing definitely helps with the circulation of money in the economy and boosts demand, but that does not mean this facility should be used for ostentatious purchases and living beyond one's means.

Keeping Promises

(Circa 1940)

Shastriji joined the freedom movement at the young age of 17 on Mahatma Gandhi's call to the youth of the nation. After a few years, he got married to my mother, Lalitaji.

During the freedom movement, Shastriji used to be jailed by the British like other freedom fighters. While in jail, he used to be very concerned about the family and particularly his wife Lalita. With three young children to take care of, my mother was not keeping good health those days. Lal Bahadur Shastri wrote a letter to her that she should drink a glass of milk every day. My mother could not afford milk for herself as she did not have enough money even to feed the family two meals a day. But she did not want to worry Shastriji with family problems and decided to drink milk in a very small glass meant for toddlers.

She wrote back to him saying that she was drinking milk everyday and that he should continue with his agitation against the foreign rule with full commitment and dedication. She said that there was no need to worry about her health. It was only after Shastriji returned from jail that he got to know from my elder sister that my mother was drinking milk in a very small glass. My father was greatly touched to see the commitment of my mother for the sake of India's freedom. When he became the Prime Minister he would always make it a point to acknowledge that his wife had greatly contributed to his success.

Wisdom Window

Some lies serve a good purpose especially like the one told by Lalita where she was lying to ensure her husband was free from household worries and could concentrate on the freedom movement.

Living within Means

(Circa 1940)

During the freedom movement, Lala Lajpat Rai had founded the Servants of the People Society. One of the objectives of the Society was to offer financial help to those freedom fighters who were not well-off and belonged to poor families. Lal Bahadur Shastri was one of them. At that time, his family comprised his wife i.e. my mother Lalita Shastri, my two elder sisters Kusum and Suman and my elder brother Hari who were all born before independence. My younger two brothers Sunil and Ashok and I were fortunate to have been born after independence when Shastriji was a Minister in Uttar Pradesh.

My father used to receive 50 rupees from the Servants of the People Society every month to meet household expenses. He would normally be very concerned

about the family while in jail and once wrote a letter to my mother wanting to know if 50 rupees from the Society were being received on time and whether the amount was sufficient to meet the household expenses.

Lalita Shastriji replied that she was receiving the money on time every month and the amount was more than sufficient to meet the needs of the family. Rather, she said, she spent only 40 rupees and saved 10 rupees every month. Shastriji immediately wrote to the Servants of the People Society that his family needs were being met with 40 rupees and the financial help to him may be reduced to 40 rupees a month and the balance 10 rupees may be given to some other needy freedom fighter.

Wisdom Window

Shastri believed in strong fiduciary management and in managing the corpus fund efficiently. He believed in widespread dispersal of available funds. When he came to know his family had some excess funds, he immediately thought of dispersing it to the needy.

Today, the more powerful people at higher echelons want to make themselves more comfortable and secure more and more for themselves, even if this comes at the cost of others in the organization.

Courage v/s Tradition

(Circa 1940)

My mother Lalita Shastri, as a young wife of Shastriji, also jumped into the freedom movement in her own way. She motivated and gathered a few women of her age to go around and educate people, particularly women, about the need for the British to leave India. They would quote what Mahatma Gandhi and other senior leaders of that time would say.

Mahatma Gandhi called for Swadeshi movement which struck a chord with the people of the country. Gandhiji appealed to the people to shun the use of foreign articles. Lalita Shastri, while going around with her team of young women, found a shop selling foreign goods in Allahabad. She demanded that the shopkeeper stop selling foreign goods. The shop keeper said that she was wearing imported bangles and that he would stop selling foreign articles provided she removed her bangles. Lalita Shastri was in a fix as bangles in India amongst Hindu women are

symbolic of being a married woman. Initially she didn't know what to say or do. But within seconds she mustered courage and removed her bangles and told the shop owner that now he should also remove imported material from his shop.

About 20 women along with Lalitaji started shouting slogans and the shop owner was compelled to give assurance that thereafter he would not sell foreign material.

It was a great achievement for my mother who showed grit and determination to tackle a difficult situation. When Shastriji got to know about this incident, he complimented her and said that she should be more involved with the freedom movement.

This anecdote speaks volumes about Lalita Shastri. Her actions and deeds gave tremendous strength to Lal Bahadur Shastri who always acknowledged her contribution to his success. She was never a hurdle to what Shastriji wanted to do, rather a strong support.

Wisdom Window

Often women are more courageous than men. When they are nurtured in an open environment, they make their own rules.

Lalita was offered such an environment by Shastri, so when the test came, she did not superstitiously believe that breaking bangles would bring about harm to her husband. She valiantly stood for the principle she was fighting for and discarded the tradition and got rid of the fear it would have evoked in women of that time.

Putting others before Self

(Circa 1956)

Life as a public figure in India is a roller-coaster ride and no one can predict when the going would become tough. I was just seven years old when a rail accident occurred in Tamil Nadu or Madras state as it was known then. Shastriji felt morally responsible for this and opted to resign as Railway Minister. He went to Pt. Nehru to tender his resignation in an official car but on his way back home, took public transport. Other changes that soon followed were that the security guards were withdrawn and we had to move to a much smaller accommodation from 1, Motilal Nehru Place (then 1 York Place) to 16 Queen Victoria Road, now known as Dr. Rajendra Prasad Marg. Shastriji's salary was also substantially reduced

as he was no longer a Minister.

One day he asked me if I felt bad at not being a Minister's son any more. I responded by saying it was not so as the family would now get more time with him than in the past. I obviously assumed that he would be less busy without a ministerial responsibility. Unfortunately this did not happen because my father became busier after relinquishing office. The second General Elections were approaching fast and Pandit Nehru gave him lot of organizational responsibilities. His tours around the country became more frequent and longer and he would hardly spend any time with us despite our complaints off and on. I remember not meeting him at times for a week or ten days at a stretch. This continued till he breathed his last as India's Prime Minister on 11th January 1966 in Tashkent.

In retrospect, I keep wondering why it was necessary for him to ask me how I felt after his resignation at a tender age of 7. A few reasons come to my mind which could be that he had seen difficult times himself and perhaps wanted to provide some comforts to his children. He resigned in the month of November and so the next few months were pretty cold. The electricity consumption was reduced as we were told not to use room heaters. The second reason I think could have been that he wanted to assess whether his children could live in unfavourable conditions and the third could have been his general concern to make people physically comfortable. I say this because whenever we had guests or visitors coming over to the house, he would make sure that they were as comfortable as possible. He would ascertain from the guests what kind of food they ate and ensured with my mother that the dishes of their liking were cooked. He would personally supervise the room where the guests would be staying to see that everything was in order.

I also remember that when my second sister was getting married, the bridegroom's party wanted non-vegetarian food to be served. The baraat was coming from Allahabad and therefore lodging and boarding had to be arranged by us. Even though Shastriji was not keen to serve non-vegetarian food at the reception of the baraat at our residence, 1, Motilal Nehru Place, he arranged for food of their choice in the janwasa (place meant for the bridegroom's party to stay).

Wisdom Window

Lal Bahadur Shastri was an extremely well-adjusted person and wanted to set an example by coming back in a tonga after resigning from his post. Having said that, he did not assume or take for granted that others would be like him. So he gave allowance to others as illustrated by him in enquiring about his son's comfort levels while staying in a smaller house and by making arrangements for the baraat to enjoy non-vegetarian food at the janwasa.

Organizational Skills

(Circa 1959)

Lal Bahadur Shastri would normally not forget what he needed to do during the course of the day. He had no formal education in management but had great skill in organizing himself and his work schedule.

Shastriji would keep noting down various issues and points on small slips of paper which he would carry in his pocket. Before going to bed he would take out these slips and delete those which had been covered during the day. He would note down the unattended issues in his small red diary for following up the following day. He thus ensured that he did not forget what was necessary and what required action.

Wisdom Window

One does not need to have a formal training in management to know about the little tools that can increase efficiency.

One of the tools mentioned here is a 'Things to do' list. I have seen many successful people carry such a list in their pocket. No matter how good our memory is there is always a possibility that one or two things might slip out.

The advantage of having such a written list is that it helps us become more efficient, more professional, and helps us prioritize our tasks. The habit of writing tasks down also ensures that we don't leave things to memory and have before us a written list of all commitments made.

Sartorial Simplicity

(Circa 1960)

In winters, Shastriji would wear his khadi woollen coat even on important occasions whereas other ministers wore expensive pashmina and other luxurious materials. The family, particularly my elder sister once got a black pashmina coat tailored for him and requested Shastriji that as a Minister he should wear more expensive clothes. Shastriji would not agree to this and continued wearing his old coats.

Once while he was going to Calcutta, my elder two sisters quietly put that black pashmina coat in his suitcase. After he reached Calcutta and was getting ready to go for a formal dinner, he realized that the old coat which he was carrying had the dry cleaning odour as it had come perhaps from the drycleaner the same day. Shastriji had no choice but to wear the expensive black pashmina coat. Pandit Nehru happened to be at that dinner and noticed the new pashmina coat which Shastriji was wearing. He jokingly tried to tease his Commerce Minister saying, "Lal Bahadur you are wearing pashmina so now you are trying to become fashionable." Shastriji was embarrassed and meekly said, "My wife put it in my suitcase." Pandit Nehru then gave back to him another one saying, "I hope one day she will put a pair of churidar pyjamas and sherwani in your suitcase, so thet you start wearing that also and do away with the old fashioned clothes."

Despite this Lal Bahadur Shastri continued to wear dhoti-kurta and didn't take to wearing churidar pyjama. However on Nehru's insistence he did wear churidar pyjama and sherwani at a banquet given in Rashtrapati Bhawan in honour of the Queen of England in 1961. Though after that, Shastriji continued to wear dhoti-kurta even when he went abroad as India's Prime Minister. He would often say that he never wanted to compare himself with Mahatma Gandhi but if Gandhiji could manage with a dhoti even in the coldest of countries which he visited then why could he not do the same. His admirers therefore always considered Lal Bahadur Shastri as a real follower of the Mahatma.

Wisdom Window

Shastri's sartorial habits showed that he was a son of the soil. He was not comfortable in changing his ethnic Indian attire to the quasi-ethnic pyjama. He had deliberated on his choices, was firm about them and was not ready to give in to social pressures.

Shastri did not believe in meeting standards - he was setting them.

Self-Help Training

(Circa 1960)

Shastriji would always want us to keep our rooms tidy and clean. In fact, whenever he would walk into our room and find trash lying on the floor and books scattered, he would pick up the bits and arrange our books properly. We would be embarrassed to see him do this and would learn to keep our things in the right place. This was his way of teaching tidiness to us.

He was self-reliant and would do his chores himself, including polishing his shoes. He would normally wash his clothes and would go in the lawn to hang them dry. This is what he taught us as well. Since he himself would set an example by doing his own things, we had no problem in following him.

Once he got to know from my mother that I shouted at one of the servants for not bringing my shoes on time as I was getting late to school. Shastriji sent a message that he would like to see me in the evening after he returned from office.

As I knew that my mother had complained, I was a little worried over the prospect of being scolded by my father. But as usual, all he told me was that thereafter I should not bother the servants for these petty things as he would himself bring the shoes on time for me. I apologized and said this would never happen again.

Shastriji had great regard for the dignity of labour. He never subscribed to the idea of 'servants' being ordered to do menial and petty work.

Wisdom Window

Shastri took pride in doing his own chores. He wanted to inculcate the same pride in every level of society. To him all chores were important and needed to be carried out in the best possible manner.

A couplet from the renowned Hindi poet Neeraj is very apt here:
Aadmi ko aadmi banane ke liye, chotti si ek prem kahani chahiye, Kagaz pe likhne wali roshnai nahi, aankhon mein thoda sa paani chahiye.
(In English it means: A man needs love in his heart to remain human. Knowledge is not everything. A shadow of compassion in one's eyes makes him a complete human being.)

That shadow of compassion shone in Shastri's eyes.

So concerned was he about the menial staff that served him that it would be apt to commemorate his death anniversary on 11th January as Service Day when we honour our house help and others who serve us.

Pocket Money

(Circa 1961)

I was in Class 8 and my father was the Home Minister in Nehru's cabinet. I had the habit of saving money which I would receive on festivals like Diwali, Holi etc. It was customary in the family for elders to bless us with small amounts of money on such occasions. I would spend a small portion and keep the balance in a money bank given to me by my mother Lalita Shastri. My brothers, on the other hand, did not save and would spend all that they got. Saving money was a trait that I had learnt from Shastriji. Over a period of time, I saved about seventy rupees and thought of saving Rs. 100/- so that I could tell my father about it who would be happy to see my saving habit.

My brothers and some friends would often tease me as a miser. This would hurt me no end and made me wonder what to do. One afternoon, I was so upset that I took seventy rupees into the toilet and flushed it away. One of my younger brothers complained to my mother and she was furious. She called me to say that the matter would be reported to Shastriji when he would return home in the evening after office. I was very scared since I was well aware that Shastriji did not like wasting even a single paisa. May be because he was born poor, he had seen very difficult days. During the freedom movement, he used to get financial assistance of Rs. 50/- from the Servants' of the People Society to meet the household expenses. He understood the value of money and losing seventy rupees would surely annoy him. Later in the evening when Shastriji returned home, my mother told him about it and I was summoned. My father had never beaten me for any mischief or offence until then but I was pretty sure that for this blunder I would get much more than just a usual reprimand.

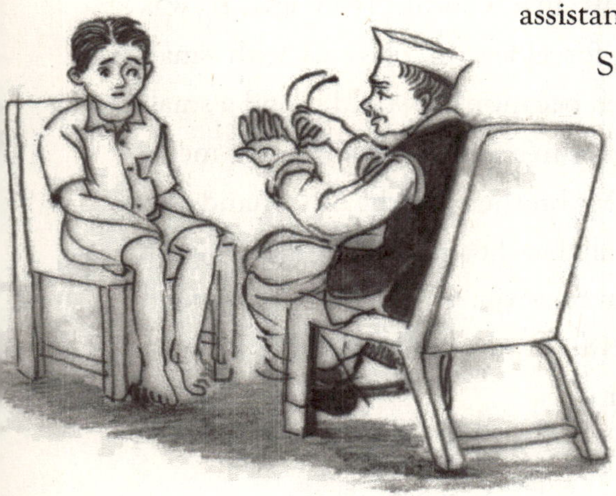

To my dismay, Shastriji asked me to sit in a nearby chair. Since he had never raised his hand on me in the past, I was wondering why he was asking me to take a seat. My head was down and I couldn't even look into his eyes. Suddenly, I heard his polite and affectionate voice asking me why I flushed the money away. I told him that I wanted to prove that I wasn't a miser. I was saving the money in fact because he had taught me to do so.

Shastriji looked at me and said, "Anil, you could have proven this by adopting a sensible method. The best way would have been to give away the money to a poor and needy person. This would have proved that you were not a miser and at the same time would have got kudos for being a kind-hearted young boy." I realized my mistake and apologized to him. I was crying profusely. When I think of this incident, I realize that had he beaten me, it would not have had the desired impact. I surely would not have wept.

Wisdom Window

Lal Bahadur believed in cracking the whip only if the mistake had not been committed by then. If the mistake had already been committed, then it made sense to help the errant person learn from his mistake rather than stun him with anger.

Another useful point which gets highlighted is that one should not whip up jealousy by bragging about one's riches or lifestyle amongst the less privileged. In fact, highlighting your problems in front of them helps reduce their jealousy.

Anil Shastri was bandying his savings in front of his siblings, buying goodies like cola and ice-cream and not sharing them with his brothers/sisters. That's why his brothers Ashok and Sunil, and niece Neerja kept teasing him and calling him 'kanjoos, makkhi choos'(miser). They were jealous not only of his savings but also of his ability to save. Anil Shastri got agitated and flushed his money as he did not know how to handle jealousy.

Time Management

(Circa 1961)

I recollect that a family friend from UK, Ms. Jean Helen Scot stayed with us in our house for a week. During her stay, the family was to visit the then President of India Dr. S Radhakrishnan. My father kept reminding us about the need to be there on time. Shastriji decided to take Ms. Scot along as well. We reached on time for the President's appointment. Ms. Scot observed that Indians were really punctual when it was absolutely necessary. Her experience was that in the normal course they would be 10 – 15 minutes late for an occasion but Indians would rarely miss a train or a flight or an examination or interview. My father was punctual too but for social gatherings he would not unnecessarily stress himself to reach on time, if a few minutes delay did not matter.

It goes to show that though Lal Bahadur Shastri had an excellent sense of time management, he was very practical too.

Wisdom Window

Jean made a good observation that for important events or meetings we are not late, though we tend to be late otherwise. This means it is not our innate nature to be late.

There are other reasons for our being late. VIPs and chief guests in India often do not arrive on time. One reason for their arriving late could be also that they do not wish to wait for other guests (who would come late) to arrive.

However in case you as a leader/chief guest are going to reach late, it is your duty to inform the waiting staff/organizers about the delay by either calling or messaging them. This will demonstrate to others that you value your time as well as theirs. Also, this will give a message to those waiting that you are a man of your word and will help you distinguish yourself in the professional world.

Westerners do not like to be kept waiting without being informed as they feel their time is not being valued. On the other hand reaching much before time is considered too keen or aggressive in the West.

Punctuality

(Circa 1962)

Shastriji was a punctual person and taught us also to be on time too. Once he was going out of station on a special plane and checked with me the previous evening if I would be interested in coming along. I happily agreed since the following day was a school holiday. He said he would leave the house at 8 o'clock in the morning as the take-off was scheduled at 8.30. Since I could not get ready on time, I tried getting to the airport in another car. By the time I reached, it was 8.35 am. The doors of the plane were closed and the engines were running. Although I was just 5 minutes late, Shastriji did not wait for me and took off and I was left behind. I felt very embarrassed and wept profusely at the airport itself.

In the evening when Shastriji came back, my mother

Lalita Shastri was annoyed with him and said that he could have waited for just 5 minutes instead of leaving me behind. All he said was, “If I didn't do that, how would Anil ever learn to be punctual.”

This was a big lesson for me and to date, I do my best to be punctual at all times.

Wisdom Window

This anecdote is very vital for understanding the importance of punctuality in management. Through one master stroke, Lal Bahadur Shastri not only taught his son the importance of punctuality but also demonstrated to everybody around him – his colleagues, driver, airport staff, etc and left them with a useful lesson to pass on to their colleagues, friends and family.

Patience Pays

(Circa 1961)

When Shastriji took over as Home Minister in 1961, the country was faced with the language problem in Assam. The situation was explosive in the Bengali-speaking Cachar district where the natives thought that the Assamese language was being imposed upon them. There was police firing in Silchar followed by a number of deaths. Emotions were running high when Home Minister Lal Bahadur Shastri decided to go to Cachar.

All the way from the banks of the Barak River to the district headquarters at Silchar, there were young boys and girls standing on either side of the road absolutely silent, but with placards of protest in their hands. It was the most effective way of silent demonstration. And at the Circuit

House in Silchar, the leaders of the Movement waited to give vent to their pent-up feelings. But they waited in vain because Shastriji first visited the hospital and spoke to those who had been wounded in the police firing. Then he went to the jail and met some of those who had been imprisoned. He even managed to meet and speak a few words of sympathy to relatives of some of those killed in the firing. And it was quite late at night when he finally landed up at the Circuit House and found quite a few people assembled there. Shastriji listened to each one, with the result that by the middle of the night the feelings of bitterness and animosity had been considerably dispelled.

Wisdom Window

The Assam anecdote shows that many a time, delay helps in diffusing the passion and calming people down. Thereafter when Shastri patiently heard the gathered people, it helped in gaining their confidence.

Of course as a manager, you should also know when and how to use delaying as a tactic. When one makes people wait it should be for a good reason and without making the waiting parties feel small.

Shastri in his native wisdom knew that he should attend to the victims first and the protestors later. And that is why he went to the hospital first, making the reason for the delay well-justified.

Non-Attention Seeking Personality

(Circa 1962)

Shastriji's humility was one of the key sources of his strength. He used to say that from his childhood, he was attracted by one of the verses of Guru Nanak Dev, "Nanak, nanhe hi raho, jalse nanhi doob, Aur rukh sookh jayenge, doob khoob ki khoob (Nanak, be small like the little blade of grass, when the other plants wither and die, the grass will continue to remain green)."

Once as Home Minister, Shastriji was in Calcutta and had to take the flight back to Delhi. It was the evening rush hour, and there was little hope of his making the long journey to Dum Dum Airport in time for the flight to Delhi. The Commissioner of police said that he would send a pilot car with a siren ahead, so that the Minister could have a clear road. But Shastriji immediately and firmly declined the offer. When people wondered why he had declined this offer, Shastriji said that the police car would go ahead making a loud noise with the siren, and everyone would think that some big man was driving down, and then they would feel let down to see 'what a small man' had come along – 'Kya cheez chali aiyee hai'.

Wisdom Window

Times have changed since Shastri, in fact they have deteriorated. Now VVIP movements not only cause inconvenience but also sometimes injure a few in the process. Some security concerns are understandable but most times, VVIPs tend to use their office to claim privileges at the cost of the common man.

Shastri believed that a great man was one who did not draw attention to himself but put his head down and worked tirelessly. He would rather let his results build his stature.

Simple Living, High Thinking

(Circa 1961 - 1963)

When Shastriji was the Union Home Minister, my two younger brothers and I were studying in St. Columbus' School, New Delhi. We would go to school in a tonga (horse carriage) whereas our friends in the same school used to be driven in cars. Their fathers were Government officials and some of them, in fact, were working under my father in the Home Ministry. We used to feel bad that though we were the Home Minister's sons, we had no car for school. One day all three of us decided to take up this matter with Shastriji.

When Shastriji returned home late evening, he was surprised to find us awake. We asked him why could we not have a car to drive us to school even though we were the Home Minister's children. He, as usual, smiled and said that he didn't own a car and all he could do was to provide a government car for us. This made us immensely happy. But he cautioned that this facility would be available to us as long as he was a Minister. Once he was out of office we would again be going to school in a tonga. We realized it would perhaps be worse switching over to tonga after having commuted by car. We, therefore, ultimately preferred to go to school by tonga.

Today, we realize that our decision as children was not wrong. I have no difficulty in accommodating and adjusting in an unfavourable situation which I owe to my father.

Wisdom Window

Lal Bahadur was very down-to-earth and wanted his kids also to be like that. Perhaps he made the offer in such a way that it was shot down by the kids themselves.

In the course of our discussion, Anil further revealed that a log book for car use was carefully maintained. At the end of the month, the private-use-amount was calculated and paid by Shastri to the government. He used to make his government officials aware of this practice so that they would also follow suit.

French President Charles De Gaulle was also a stickler for honesty. He would even pay for postage stamps that he had used personally to set an example for the not-so-honest French government officials.

After Nehru, Who?

(Circa 1961)

Jawaharlal Nehru was the first Prime Minister of India and was a towering personality. He ruled for 17 years and had almost become indispensable. After his illness in January 1964, most political commentators started asking the question "After Nehru, Who?" There were foreigners like Michael Brecher and Welles Hangen and some Indian authors who posed the same question as to who would succeed Jawaharlal Nehru.

Some of the names which started doing the rounds for this coveted post were Morarji Desai, S.K. Patil, Kamraj, Indira Gandhi, Lal Bahadur Shastri, Y.B. Chavan and T.T. Krishnamachari. Shastriji's leadership style and his tact to deal with people made him a likeable and popular leader. His acceptability in the party was high but was shy and would shun publicity. He was also not perceived to be ambitious. Rather, he was seen as a politician who would not hanker for power. Although the political commentators of that time saw these traits of Shastriji going against him in the race to the office of Prime Minister, these very qualities made him the unanimous choice as the leader of the party. The Congress leaders of that time were fully aware that nobody could match the stature of Nehru so the party might as well have somebody whose acceptability was high and could take everybody along. They found in Shastri the right leader to lead the party and the nation after Nehru.

Wisdom Window

In fact history has shown again and again that the successor anointed is often the one against or for whom the opinion is not polarized.

Martin Luther King was not among the main contenders to lead the black equality movement in America. In fact he was hardly known. But the other main contenders cancelled each other out because just as they had support groups, there were groups to whom they were completely unacceptable. Which is why, due to his non-controversial candidature which no one was vehemently opposed to, Martin Luther King was declared the leader of the black movement.

The race always does not go to the most flamboyant of runners. It also does not go often to the most popular choice. Shastri was the most non-controversial among the contenders and acceptable to all and thus made the Prime Minister of India.

Family Man

(Circa 1964)

At St. Columbus' School it was common practice for parents to collect the report card of their wards on the dates specified by the school in the 1950s and 60s. My father always made it a point to personally collect my report card from the class teacher. He did this while he was a Minister in the Union Cabinet. This, of course, was greatly appreciated by the school authorities. In fact the class teacher would quote me as exemplary to some of those students whose parents would not care to visit the school to collect the report card of their children.

In June 1964 my father became the country's Prime Minister. The second term examination was in September and the report card was ready just before the autumn break which began before Dusshera. Parents were advised to collect the report card of their wards before the school closed for the autumn break. Shastriji told me that he would come to the school to collect the report. It was nothing unusual for me. However, when he turned up at the school with minimal security, he got down at the gate itself and told the driver to park the car outside. The gate keeper insisted that the car could be parked

inside but Shastriji refused to oblige him. He told Shastriji that after all he was now India's Prime Minister. Shastriji responded by saying that he had come to the school not as Prime Minister but as Anil Shastri's father and would like to be treated as any other parent.

My class XI-B was on the first floor and he climbed up along with me to enter the class. My class teacher Reverend Brother Tynon was taken aback to see him and politely said that there was no need for him to come to collect the report card as he could have sent somebody else for this purpose. Shastriji said that he was doing this all along and will continue to do so. Brother Tynon said but he was now the Prime Minister! Shastriji smilingly responded, "Brother Tynon, I have not changed after becoming the Prime Minister but it seems you have."

Wisdom Window

Shastri went to the school to get the report card to indicate to his children that being Prime Minister did not mean he stopped shouldering the responsibilities of a father. He wanted to reassure them that despite his work load, their father was there for them just as before.

Also by this gesture of his, the children knew that their progress was being monitored and hence they continued to take their studies seriously.

He always identified himself with the common man and by going to the school for the report card he proved that he was no different from any other parent whose child was studying at St. Columbus.

Message in a Car

(Circa 1964)

Lal Bahadur Shastri did not own a car until he became Prime Minister of India. As children, we brothers and sisters always wanted to have a car for the family but Shastriji never obliged us. So I made my request of us owning a car when he became the Prime Minister.

One evening he called us and said that he had decided to buy a car and we were thrilled. He requested one of his staff members to find out his bank balance and the price of a new car. His bank balance was about Rs. 7,000 and the price of a Fiat car at that time was about Rs. 12,000. We were shocked that as India's Prime Minister he had only Rs. 7,000. However, Shastriji did not disappoint us and applied for a loan from the Punjab National Bank as Prime Minister and bought the car for us. After a year, he died and the loan remained unpaid.

Although the Government offered to waive off the loan, my mother decided not to accept the offer and repaid the loan from her monthly pension amount. This loan was repaid in 3-4 years after Shastriji's death. I am indeed proud to have used the car because for me it meant much more than just a car. With it are associated values and memories which I will always cherish.

The car has been kept for public display at the Lal Bahadur Shastri Memorial in Delhi. And several hundred people visit to see for themselves this car which was purchased against loan by a Prime Minister. It is one of the star attractions at the museum.

Wisdom Window

Shastri might be among the rare heads of state in the world history whose bank balance was two-third the cost of an ordinary car.

His leadership quality is proven by the fact that his closest follower, his wife Lalita, donned his mantle. She walked in his footsteps and insisted on repaying the car loan taken by Shastri. Lalita demonstrated that she subscribed to Shastri's value system even though in the beginning she used to be a little critical of his utmost honesty.

Personal integrity is a trait for which Lal Bahadur is remembered even today after many decades of his death. Whenever a scam or a corrupt practice comes to light, even today the media and the public cite this incident.

Devious Driving Licence

(Circa 1964)

When my father became India's Prime Minister in 1964, I was 15 years old and was not eligible for a driving license. The minimum age for obtaining a driving license was 18 years and I was thus short by 3 years.

I had learnt driving on the quiet at the age of 14 itself. The afternoons were perfect for me to take the car out for driving practice on Akbar Road which hardly had any traffic at that time. The family members would be resting then and my father would be away to office. My elder brother, who was 10 years older than me, was working in a private company in Madras (now Chennai). On my insistence, one of the drivers agreed to teach me the basics of car driving. As I was fairly young, it took very little time for me to perfect the art of driving a car.

When I was confident of driving the car alone, I wanted to then possess a driving license and so requested my father's Additional Private Secretary Shri Kailash Narayan to help me in getting one. He took immediate action and the license was delivered to me at the Prime Minister's house the same day. I proudly told this to Shastriji when he returned in the evening hoping that he would be pleased to see my license. He was not angry but seemed a little hurt and upset. The next morning, he sent for Kailash Narayan and told him that it was very wrong on his part to have done an illegal act as a personal staff member of the Prime Minister.

He also sent a message to the Home Ministry to take the RTO officials to task. Shastriji said that the law of the land was openly flouted in the Prime Minister's house itself and that was perhaps the reason he was so hurt when I showed him the driving license the previous evening.

He told the officials that the license was issued in the name of the person who was not eligible in terms of age and secondly it was issued and delivered without any driving test. Shri Kailash Narayan and the RTO officials were ashamed of their mis-judgment and profusely apologised to the Prime Minister for their serious act of omission.

Wisdom Window

Shastri believed that the laws of the land were to be honoured and followed by everyone, more so by people in power. Nobody was above the law and the law did not make exceptions for anyone, whosoever they might be.

He also wanted to send a strong message that bending rules to appease higher ups and their wards was not acceptable. This is why he took corrective action immediately when he saw the law being flexed in this instance. He believed that those who took law in their own hands were just as culpable as those who abetted those people.

emulate him. It makes no difference to me what the foreign dignitaries think as long as they know that the Indian Prime Minister is travelling in a car which is made in India. "

Wisdom Window

By using the Cadillac, Nehru was bringing himself and his nation on par with his guests. To Shastri, it really did not matter as to what he had, what mattered was what he was.

Today's generation needs to learn to be comfortable in its skin rather than seeking identity through expensive brands bought in glitzy malls.

My Grandmother

Lal Bahadur Shastri was not even two when he lost his father. The entire burden of bringing him up fell on his mother i.e. my grandmother Ram Dulari Devi. Since my grandfather Shri Sharda Prasad died when he was just 28 years old, my grandmother's age at that time would have been 23 years. It is difficult to imagine how at that young age, she took upon herself to bring up her son Lal Bahadur and his elder sister Kailashi Devi who was 4 years old. Besides, she was also expecting another child in a few months' time. The third child happened to be a girl and was named Sundari Devi. Shastriji thus had one elder sister and one younger.

Despite all odds, as a young widow, Ram Dulari Devi managed to bring up her children and endeavoured all along to make them into good human beings and honest and upright citizens of this great nation. She also succeeded in her mission of marrying both her daughters into good families and their children led fairly happy lives holding responsible positions. In fact, Sundari Devi's son was selected in the IAS and was allotted the Bihar cadre.

My father, Lal Bahadur was brought up so well by his mother that he did extremely well in his studies. He was fluent in five languages viz Hindi, English, Sanskrit, Urdu and Persian. He got the degree of 'Shastri' from Kashi Vidyapeeth, Varanasi. He joined the freedom movement and after independence, became the Prime Minister of India in 1964. The day he took oath of office as Prime Minister, my grandmother was in Varanasi. She was doing her *pooja* at the banks of the mighty Ganges when horde of press correspondents rushed to her to congratulate on her son becoming the Prime Minister. They asked her about her expectations of her son. All that she replied was, "My only advice to my son is that he should never ever compromise with the dignity and honour of his countrymen." Tears of joy rolled down her cheeks and the same evening she took the train to New Delhi to be with her son.

Wisdom Window

I recall a research undertaken by Howard Gardner which identifies "early markers" that define future leaders. He observes that leaders are those who experienced failure or adversity early in their lives.

Many great leaders have lost their fathers in childhood. This circumstance, though unfortunate, makes the child responsible and mature. He often begins to resemble the guardian of the family, kind of standing in for the father who is no more. Shastri also perhaps donned the mantle of the guardian. And so well that one day he rose to become the guardian of the nation.

3rd January
(1966)

A few days before Shastriji left for Tashkent, I requested for a photograph with him. Surprisingly, I had no exclusive photograph snapped with him until then. He called my mother and three of us had ourselves photographed. He even gave his autograph with his good wishes on the print which I have treasured.

Very few people know that I was to accompany my father to Tashkent since my mother, due to some unforeseen reason, was not going along with him. I do not know what happened and my programme was suddenly cancelled just one day before his departure. I felt extremely bad as I had told all my friends that I was going to the Soviet Union which apparently was going to be my first visit to that great country. My father called me and told me not to get disappointed and promised to take me along on his forthcoming visit to the United States. Though it was some consolation to me, I was depressed and unhappy.

In fact, I did not even see him off at the Delhi Airport even though the entire family had been to the Airport to bid goodbye and wish him success at Tashkent. It was the 3rd of January, 1966 when Shastriji was about to leave at 7.00 in the morning for his ill-fated trip to Tashkent. I was awake tossing in my bed. He passed by my bed kissing me with a smile and that was the last I saw of my father.

Wisdom Window

We should not broadcast our plans to others. As, if those plans don't materialize, our sense of disappointment is deeper. We are also seen as less able by those with whom we have shared our "unsuccessful" plans.

Also, one must never let any emotionally important moment go by. Given the unpredictability of life, that could well be the last special moment spent with that significant person.

Values to Enhance our Interpersonal Relationships

If your emotional abilities aren't in hand, if you don't have self-awareness, if you are not able to manage your distressing emotions, if you can't have empathy and have effective relationships, then no matter how smart you are, you are not going to get very far.

- Daniel Goleman

Lal Bahadur Shastri exhibited genuine concern and compassion for all. His interpersonal skills were very refined. No doubt he was loved and cherished by people from all walks of life and across all age groups.

The following anecdotes give us great insight into how we should conduct ourselves to be able to influence others effectively. Lal Bahadur Shastri handled several crises sensitively and sure-footedly without burning bridges or incensing people. This is the true hallmark of a courageous leader who always keeps others above self.

Strong Work Ethic

(Circa 1945)

Elections to the provincial assembly were held in UP at the end of 1945. The Congress got an overwhelming majority and Shri Govind Ballabh Pant was unanimously elected as leader of the Congress Legislature Party and became the Chief Minister. Pantji was also member of the Congress Working Committee, the highest decision making body in the organization. He enjoyed the trust of Shri Jawaharlal Nehru.

Govind Ballabh Pant needed a parliamentary secretary who was both able and trustworthy. He therefore chose Lal Bahadur Shastri. Shastriji vindicated Pantji's expectation of him in the discharge of his legislative responsibilities. In the process, he came pretty close to Pantji and after independence, he was appointed in his Cabinet as UP's Home & Transport Minister. Pantji described Shastriji as 'likeable, hard-working, devoted, trustworthy and non-controversial'.

Pantji was in the habit of working late in the office and so was Lal Bahadur. The other Ministers and Parliamentary

Secretaries would normally pack up for the day at a decent hour of the evening. Shastriji would invariably end up travelling back home from office in Pantji's car which brought them closer politically.

Wisdom Window

The true mark of a leader is two-fold:
One, a leader creates opportunities.
Two, he fully taps every opportunity.

In this anecdote, to become Govind Ballabh Pant's next in command was an opportunity and an honour for Shastri and he capitalized on this opportunity by increasing his proximity to his boss, even if it meant working late hours.

Research shows that working as late as your boss makes you bond with your boss better and brings you power.

Of course in the changed scenario today it is not suggested that the managers necessarily have to work long hours with their bosses. What is now expected from them is to finish the targeted assignment irrespective of the number of hours.

Crisis Management

(Circa 1950)

When Lal Bahadur Shastri was UP's Home Minister, he officially went to watch a test match between India and England. One enclosure was earmarked for university students. For some reason, a scuffle ensued between the students and UP police posted at the Green Park Cricket Stadium.

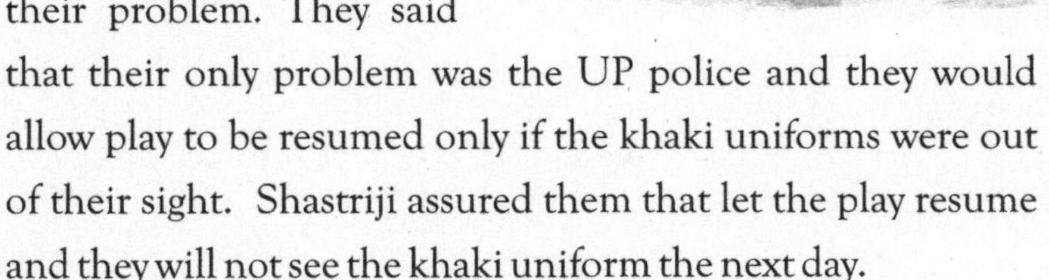

The students were shouting and yelling and because of the commotion, the play had to be suspended. Shastriji went up to the students and enquired about their problem. They said that their only problem was the UP police and they would allow play to be resumed only if the khaki uniforms were out of their sight. Shastriji assured them that let the play resume and they will not see the khaki uniform the next day.

The following day the cricket match commenced on time and within a few minutes the students again started shouting. Shastriji went up to them and enquired what was wrong.

They said, "We had been assured yesterday there would not be any police today but they are present in much larger numbers." Shastriji smilingly replied that what was agreed upon was that there won't be any policemen in khaki uniform and today, he said, "They are in white uniform!" The students laughed heartily and realized how witty Shastriji had been. They immediately withdrew their agitation and allowed the cricket match to continue.

Wisdom Window

The mark of a good leader is to diffuse a crisis and to make sure grace and decorum are maintained in the public eye. He does it in a way that does not further exacerbate the situation but improves it.

By quadrupling the police force in white uniform, Shastri not only helped retain country's respect before the visiting team but also taught the youth of India a vital lesson in retaining the flexibility to act without lying.

Purushotham Das Tandon and Pandit Nehru

(Circa 1952)

The 1952 General Elections were approaching. This was the first General Election after independence and Pt. Nehru wanted a reliable and effective political leader who was totally familiar with the organization and its people. To look after the election work he thought of Lal Bahadur Shastri who was UP's Home Minister in Pt. Govind Ballabh Pant's cabinet. This was in 1951. Panditji asked Shastriji if he would do party work to which he readily agreed. Shastriji resigned as UP's Home Minister to take over as General Secretary of All India Congress Committee. Pandit Nehru who had ideological differences with another senior political leader Purushotham Das Tandon wanted Shastriji to go and check with the latter if he had any objection to this appointment. Shastriji met Tandonji who said, "I am happy Jawahar Lal is taking a wise decision."

This goes to show that Lal Bahadur's acceptance at all levels of the Congress organization was high. This is because he knew the party and its people pretty well.

Wisdom Window

It is said that one cannot please two masters. This saying may apply to ordinary men but Shastri was certainly not ordinary. His purity of thought and action. and his non-partisan ways made even warring leaders trust him equally.

Man Management

(Circa 1958)

Although Shastriji had no formal education in management, Human Resource Management concepts came naturally to him.

Once, one of his officers came up to him and said that he was having some difficulty in understanding and carrying out the assignment given to him. The work was urgent. Anybody else in place of Shastriji would have told him to forget about it and would have given the assignment to somebody else but Shastriji spent time and made the effort to understand his problem, explain his viewpoint and suggest how he could proceed. The officer did the job in record time and to the fullest of Shastriji's satisfaction.

Wisdom Window

One of the traits of an authentic leader is to be able to understand his subordinates' problems, solve these problems and be facilitative in achieving the desired result. Shastri had empathy for his staff and juniors and sensed their needs even before they could verbalise it.

The Great Motivator

(Circa 1958)

Minoo Masani, Member of Parliament from the Swatantra Party, had known Shri Lal Bahadur Shastri for a long time since 1935. His impression of Shastriji was that of a gentlemanly figure with great humility but tremendous intelligence and talent.

Minoo Masani was introduced to Shastriji by Shri Jawaharlal Nehru at his Anand Bhavan residence in the 1930's. Thereafter during his visits to Allahabad, Shri Masani had the opportunity of meeting Lal Bahadur Shastri on several occasions. He lost touch for some time but met him again when Shastriji became a Minister in the Union Government headed by Shri Jawaharlal Nehru. When Shastriji was the minister for tourism, Minoo Masani in one of his

speeches in the Lok Sabha was critical of the Government's record and relative lack of interest in the revenue-earning field of tourism. After the debate, Shastriji asked his secretary whether he had briefed Minoo Masani before he made the speech. The official replied in the affirmative and Shastriji responded by saying, "Good. It was a critical but excellent speech and I am glad you helped him make it. Next time, keep me also informed."

Wisdom Window

Shastri knew how to balance openness with reserve so that the credibility of his department did not come under question. That is why he said to his secretary, "Next time, keep me also informed."

Chamber of Commerce

(Circa 1959)

If Shastriji succeeded as a negotiator, it was primarily because of the fact that he had the ability to appreciate the other person's point of view. He was always ready to make maximum allowance for the feelings of the other person. Of course at times, people close to him wished that he were a little firmer but his style ensured resolution of every problem that he tackled. His Special Assistant Shri Rajeshwar Prasad, IAS, recollects one example of his negotiation skills. **The text pasted below is excerpted from Rajeshwar Prasad's book on Lal Bahadur Shastri:**

"When Shastriji was Minister of Commerce and Industry, he accepted the invitation from the Chamber of Commerce in Calcutta to address an important function. The practice on such occasions was that the draft speech of the Chamber's President would be sent in advance, on the basis of which the Ministry would suggest the draft speech to the Minister. In this case, when the draft for the President's speech arrived, it contained scathing criticism of the Government's policies and the Ministry's functioning, and there were also untoward remarks about the Minister himself.

On seeing this draft, the Secretary of the Ministry, Shri S. Ranganathan (later the Comptroller and Auditor General) sent for me. He was flanked by the two Additional Secretaries in charge of Industry and Commerce, Shri L.K. Jha and Shri

K.B. Lall. The Secretary said that having invited the Minister, it was very unbecoming of the Chamber's President to launch this tirade against the Government, and that too with so much fitting and forceful reply. I pointed out that it would not be easy to get the Minister to say anything forceful, but the Secretary said that it was not just a personal matter but official policy was involved, and a firm reply must be given. Knowing the Minister's nature, I kept the tone of the speech mild, however inserted a few strong sentences here and there.

On the flight to Calcutta, Shastriji took out the draft speech prepared for him, went through it carefully, and one by one deleted all the sentences that smacked of firmness. I remonstrated and mentioned to him what the Secretary had

told me about giving a firm and forceful reply in view of the very unbecoming and vituperative speech of the Chamber's President. But Shastriji just smiled and said, "You are all big officers. When you sit behind your big tables in your big offices, you forget the trials and sorrows of the common people. But I am one of them. How can I be blind to their trials and tribulations?" "This President" he said, "do you think he is mad that he should have spat poison in this manner? Countless number of times he must have walked the corridors of Udyog Bhavan, knocking one door after another, but may not have found answers. And thus, driven to despair and desperation, he has given vent to his feelings of exasperation. How can I be annoyed with him? Rather, I should take pity on him." What could I say thereafter?

However, when the meeting commenced, we hoped that in the presence of the Minister, the President would have the good sense to tone down his speech. But he was a young man of about 35, and he read out all that he had written with great vehemence, and with a curl of the lip and a sneer. There was a hush when the Minister rose to reply. But Shastriji just said quietly, "Your President has spoken with great fire and fury. He is a young, fiery man, I am a mature person. So I will not attempt to emulate him, but shall confine myself to giving you the facts." Upon which, he proceeded to read out his speech in an even tone, and usual calm and dignified manner. And no sooner had he finished than we saw the amazing spectacle of member after member of that Chamber of Commerce getting up and apologizing to the Minister and repudiating their President, who sat at the head of the table looking thoroughly downcast with face almost buried in his hands."

Wisdom Window

Shastri understood the pain and agony common man goes through when he has to knock on the government's door.

The kind of vent which Shastri gave the Chamber's President is the big need of today.

Shastri also initiated administrative reforms commission to make the government more responsive to the aspirations of the people.

Today this sensitivity towards the common man seems to be lacking in both politicians and bureaucrats. Instead arrogance, inefficiency and corruption seem to be the order of the day.

Tea Party

(Circa 1960)

Pandit Nehru was a very jovial person and he would not spare anyone when he was in a good mood. Shri Gujar Mal Modi had invited Panditji, Shastriji and some other senior leaders of the Congress Party to his house in Modinagar for high tea. The party was very enjoyable and carried on till long. Panditji mischievously placed two samosas in the pocket of Shastriji. When the party was over and everyone was leaving, Panditji joked loudly in the presence of everyone that Lal Bahadur was taking away two samosas even though he had enough of them at the party.

Shastriji promptly replied, "I have kept them for two important people who will have it in the car."

Wisdom Window

'I have kept them for two important people who will have it in the car.' - most people thought these two important people were Pandit Nehru and Shastri. Little did they know that Shastri was talking about the two drivers. He knew that the meeting would go on till late and not much was available to eat outside for the drivers.

Trusting those Below the Radar

(Circa 1960)

Shastriji had respect for those whose life came in contact with his, however insignificant their position may have been. He reposed faith in their integrity and judgement. Once he was authorized by a competent body to improve the working of the administration and congress organization in a problem state. He allocated a little known Member of Parliament to such an important task. Not only that, he approved this aide's assessment of the situation in the state and accepted his suggestions for solution of the problems posed.

The sequel to this highlights another aspect of Shastriji's character and mode of functioning. The leaders of the government and organization of this state were summoned to Delhi. His (above mentioned) aide, in his inexperience and impatience, suggested that the decisions should be announced to them and directive issued to implement them. With an affectionate pat on his back, Shastriji advised him not to be impatient in matters of such importance. He assured him, however, that he would so conduct those talks that the solutions suggested by him would ultimately come from the state leaders themselves. At 10.30 in the night, Shastriji crossed over to the room in which state leaders were waiting.

At 3 am, he woke this aide, shook him out of sleep and told him that after prolonged talks, the state leaders themselves suggested the same solutions this aide had listed and Shastriji accepted them! The State leaders went back satisfied.

Wisdom Window

The first half of the anecdote shows that most recruiters hire a candidate with visible pedigree, and credentials such as a good degree, experience in good organizations. Very few recruiters are courageous enough to go for only brilliance and merit. Shastri was one such recruiter which is why he gave a chance to an insignificant member of parliament and hired him.

The second part reveals that Shastri was also an intuitive psychologist. He knew how to seed his idea in the other man's mind unobtrusively so that it took root and bore fruit.

There are several ways of planting ideas. Firstly, you need to be a patient listener. If you interrupt the other person while he is talking, he could think you have some preconceived ideas, and clamp up. So let him speak and vent his feelings, and hear him out completely. Then through your questions which could lead to solutions, weave your ideas in his thoughts, and let them flower in his mind. He will slowly start to consider these as his own. This way his ego will get satisfied which will make him more amenable to the idea and even propel him to take it further.

Raising Delicate Issues Unabashedly

(Circa 1960)

When Lal Bahadur Shastri was the Minister for Commerce & Industry, he had to decide on the location of the Heavy Electrical Plants which were to be established with Soviet aid and technical support. Quite a few State Governments were interested in setting up the plant in their own state. To ensure a fair decision in the matter, Shastriji set up a Technical Committee to make a thorough study and put up their recommendations to him. The Committee was presided over by a retired Chairman of the Railway Board, a very competent person who had exalted notions of himself.

While travelling by air to Hyderabad, the Chairman and the members of the Technical Committee happened to be on the same flight as Shastriji. Those days the planes used to be small and this one was a 44 seater pressurized turbo-prop Viscount. Being a small plane as compared to today's fleets, it was hardly possible for a passenger not to notice other passengers in the plane. The Chairman and members however passed by the Minister without a word of greeting.

That afternoon there was a big public meeting in Hyderabad and the Chairman and members of the Technical Committee were also present. The Chief Minister of Andhra Pradesh, Shri Brahmananda Reddy said in his speech that his government would make land, water and power for the Heavy Electrical Plant to be set up in the State and that Shastriji should agree to do so. There was a big applause.

Shri Lal Bahadur Shastri in his speech said that he would personally be happy if Andhra Pradesh got one of the Heavy Electrical Units but then he had constituted a Technical Committee which was competent enough to take a decision in the matter. The Committee would examine all aspects and make a fair recommendation as he had given them complete freedom.

He said, "You can be very sure that a thoroughly objective and impartial report would be submitted by the Committee. The Chairman and the Members of the Committee were travelling with me in the same flight this morning but took care to avoid greeting me lest I influenced them with my views." All present had a big laugh but the Chairman and his colleagues were very embarrassed as shared later by one of the team members.

Wisdom Window

Shastri knew how to reign in the bureaucracy. He did not react to the delicate situation immediately but waited for the right moment and then raised the point, of being ignored on the flight, in front of so many dignitaries.

Delayed response is a technique often used by successful leaders. This keeps the opponents guessing as to what the person's next move would be.

Coalition Politics

(Circa 1961)

There was a time when Congress had a coalition government in Kerala with the erstwhile Praja Socialist Party (PSP). Although Congress party's strength in the assembly was more than the PSP, as per the coalition arrangement, Shri Pattom Thannu Pillai of the PSP was leading the Government. Congress had a Deputy Chief Minister in Shri R. Sankar. There were serious differences between the two parties and Prime Minister Nehru deputed Shastriji to resolve the deadlock.

Lal Bahadur Shastri reached Trivandrum and in Raj Bhavan talked to leaders of both the parties the whole day and the whole night. It was a very exhausting process. This went on for 3 days and 3 nights. He must have listened to virtually 400 – 500 people one after the other. Although it was a tremendous

strain on him, he put forward his suggestions which were readily accepted by both the parties. His patience and perseverance paid. The bitterness between the leaders evaporated after they could speak their heart out to Shastriji.

The end result was that Pattom Thannu Pillai agreed to become the Governor of Punjab and the Congress had its Chief Minister to lead the Government.

Wisdom Window

Avoid arguments and try to win through patient hearing and well thought through actions. This is possible if you are convinced that you are right and creative enough to prove it - without arguing.

Also patient hearing gives the impression that you are in control and helps in gaining confidence of the opposing parties as was in this case. This helps in arriving at a common consensus.

Two Deputy Leaders

(Circa 1961)

After independence Jawaharlal Nehru took over as Prime Minister and Sardar Vallabh Bhai Patel was elected Deputy Leader of the Congress Parliamentary Party and was also appointed as Deputy Prime Minister. Sardar Patel died in 1950 and Maulana Abul Kalam Azad was elected as Deputy Leader of the Congress Parliamentary Party. Once bitten twice shy, Nehru did not want another Deputy Prime Minister in his cabinet. Maulana Azad thus continued as Deputy Leader and Minister for Education until his death in 1958. After his death, Pt. Govind Ballabh Pant who was the Home Minister at that time and was the senior most leader in the Parliamentary Party, was the automatic choice as Deputy Leader of the Congress Parliamentary Party.

In 1961, Pt. Govind Ballabh Pant passed away and Morarji Desai, being the senior most in the cabinet, wanted to be elected as Deputy Leader of the Congress Parliamentary Party. This was resisted by several leaders in Nehru's cabinet including T.T. Krishnamachari, Shri C. Subramaniam, Guljari Lal Nanda and Jagjivan Ram. Lal Bahadur Shastri, though succeeded Pt. Pant as Home Minister, had already declared that he was not in the race for this post. Indira Gandhi, though not in the cabinet, was not keen on Morarji Desai being elected as Deputy Leader. She expressed this to her father Pt. Jawaharlal Nehru. Panditji asked her to speak to Lal Bahadur. Shastriji found a solution. He said that the unanimity on the choice of a Deputy Leader seemed difficult and therefore suggested that instead of a Deputy Leader of the Congress Parliamentary Party, there should be two Deputy Leaders, one in the Lok Sabha and another in the Rajya Sabha. His proposal also included that the two Deputy Leaders will not be members of the Union Cabinet which was readily accepted by all senior leaders and thus the ambition of Morarji Desai to become the Deputy Leader of the Party was scuttled. Morarji, of course was not happy but had no choice than to bow in line with the unanimous acceptance of Shastriji's proposal by other senior leaders.

Wisdom Window

Take the case of Romulus.

Romulus, the founder of Rome, was the man who made laws for free existence. In order to establish a civil society in Rome, Romulus had to first kill his brother, and then consent to the killing of his partner even though, initially, he had himself chosen this partner to share the kingdom with him. Prima facie, these acts make him appear violent, ruthless and unfaithful. However, because his intention was not to grab power but to introduce socio-political equality, Romulus is lauded not denigrated. Soon after the murder of his brother and his partner, Romulus instituted a senate for consultation, followed the advice given by them, and thus laid the foundations for what we today call democracy.

Sometimes for a very good cause Lal Bahadur had to take certain "grey" steps. He was concerned that since the nation was under tremendous pressure due to a weak economy and borders being constantly under attack from Pakistan and China, it was important to create a strong centralized authority to strengthen the democracy. Having a deputy leader created the possibility of multiplicity of command and diluted the authority of the Prime Minister. So instead, Shastri suggested creating two diluted versions of deputy leaders, one each for Lok Sabha and Rajya Sabha. And by not allowing such a leader to come from the Union Cabinet he assured complete authority for the Prime Minster.

Touching Elders' Feet

(Circa 1961)

It is a culture in India to touch the feet of parents and other elders in the family as a mark of respect, especially on special occasions like festivals, religious functions and birthdays. The youngsters also take blessings by touching the feet of elders while leaving home or upon returning home. We followed the same practice in our family as well.

One evening after dinner, my father called me to his room and said that he had noticed that I was not touching the feet of elders properly. I refused to accept this but he explained that my hands went only up to the knees and not up to the feet. I was a young boy studying in class VIII and would not accept my fault easily and argued with him that I touched the feet correctly and that he might have noticed my brothers not doing so properly.

Any other father would have scolded his son but to my dismay, Shastriji touched my feet with all humility and respect and said that do try to greet your elders in the manner that he had demonstrated. I was in tears and started sobbing and asked him why he had to punish me so severely. I also asked him to pardon me for my behaviour and assured him that I would always remember in my life to touch the feet of my elders properly. Lal Bahadur Shastri's humility and non-egotistic action indelibly etched this valuable lesson in my mind which perhaps words might have failed to do.

Wisdom Window

Indian society is very hierarchical and at times, this seems hypocritical. One is expected to show respect to all his elders, even those whom he does not regard. There is indiscriminate use of 'Sir' too. A good balance would be to touch feet of grandparents, parents and revered elders only and show respect where it comes naturally.

On the other hand, western societies are far too egalitarian. In fact, the French society has become so egalitarian that most people are seeking a change. So much so that President Sarkozy in his election manifesto had promised if he were elected, he would make sure students addressed their teachers as Wu(Aap) and not Tu (Tum)!!

Mediation in Uttar Pradesh (UP)

(Circa 1960 - 63)

In the early 60's, the UP Congress was divided into two factions. One was led by Kamlapati Tripathi who was supported by Pt. Govind Ballabh Pant, Lal Bahadur Shastri and Indira Gandhi and the other faction was led by another eminent leader, C.B. Gupta.

At that time, the State Executive comprised of 21 members out of which 10 were nominated and 10 had to be elected. Both the factions put up their candidates and Kamlapati Tripathi's candidates were covertly supported by Pantji, Shastriji and Indiraji. The result was shocking for all as C.B. Gupta managed to get majority of his candidates elected. As a result, he got complete control over the UPCC Executive. Lal Bahadur Shastri at that time was Minister for Commerce and Industry in Nehru's Cabinet.

After the State Executive elections, Pt. Nehru asked Shastriji, "What should be done in UP, Lal Bahadur?" Shastriji replied, "We should make C.B. Gupta the Chief Minister." Nehru agreed and C.B. Gupta took over as Chief Minister much against the wishes of leaders who were on the side of Kamlapati Tripathi. In March 1961, Pt. Govind Ballabh Pant died as Home Minister and Shastrji was appointed as the new Home Minister.

Then came the Kamraj plan in 1963 under which 6 Union Cabinet Ministers and 6 Chief Ministers had to resign. C.B. Gupta was one of the Chief Ministers to resign. Kamlapati Tripathi wanted to succeed him but was fiercely opposed by Gupta. Nehruji again requested Shastriji to go to Lucknow and resolve the leadership issue in the state. After long and tiring consultations with various leaders, Lal Bahadur Shastri arrived at a consensus in favour of Smt. Sucheta Kriplani. She was the wife of Acharya J.B. Kriplani, a great Socialist leader of that time who was ideologically opposed to Jawaharlal Nehru. Sucheta Kriplani thus became the Chief Minister.

Then the new cabinet had to be formed. Again it was difficult for Sucheta Kriplani to form her Council of Ministers because of the two warring factions wanting more representation from their respective camps. The High Command asked Lal Bahadur Shastri to help Sucheta Kriplani in constituting her Council of Ministers. It was on October 11, 1963 that Shastriji was able to prepare an agreed list of Ministers and Deputy Ministers for a composite cabinet of 21 members - 16 Cabinet Ministers and 5 Deputy Ministers. This was approved by the Central Parliamentary Board in New Delhi on the same day. The list included representatives of both C.B. Gupta, Kamlapati Tripathi along with two new faces recommended by Sucheta Kriplani. This agreement on cabinet formation was not easy and it required a fortnight of hectic political activities in New Delhi and Lucknow. It took the wisdom of a leader like Lal Bahadur

Shastri to successfully mediate through a deadlock.

Wisdom Window

Shastri always believed in being fair. Even though C.B. Gupta was his political adversary, on being asked by Nehru, Shastri endorsed C.B. Gupta's candidature for the chief ministership of UP. Of course as a seasoned politician, through this move, he successfully eliminated dissidence in UP assembly.

After Kamraj Plan came into effect, C.B. Gupta was one of the six Chief Ministers to go. Shastri ensured that UP state was back under Nehru's control by installing his key people in the cabinet.

Keeping Enemies Closer

(Circa 1963)

After Lal Bahadur Shastri resigned under the Kamaraj Plan, he was looking after the Congress affairs in UP. There was a change of government and Sucheta Kripalani took over as the Chief Minister. Raghukul Tilak, a leading politician of those days had gone over to Sucheta's residence to offer his good wishes on her becoming the Chief Minister. She was busy trying to form her Cabinet. On seeing him, she suddenly brightened up and said that she wanted a favour. She said that Lal Bahadur Shastri was insisting on somebody to be taken into her Cabinet which she was resisting as she believed that the person was a troublemaker. She requested Raghukulji to persuade Shastriji not to do so.

When Raghukul Tilak met Lal Bahadur Shastri, the latter said that Suchetaji does not realize that the person he was recommending would be a bigger troublemaker if he remained outside the Cabinet. It was therefore in the interest of smooth functioning of the Government that he believed that the concerned politician would be less troublesome if he was within the Cabinet.

When Raghukul Tilak conveyed this to Sucheta Kriplani, she accepted there was a lot of sense in what Lal Bahadurji said and the person in question was taken by her in the Cabinet.

Wisdom Window

Andrew Johnson, Abraham Lincoln's successor as President of the USA, isolated Ulysses S. Grant, a troublesome member of the government. He then forced him out. This enraged Grant, who then worked hard to build his base in the Republican Party and went on to become the next President.

It is often better to keep such troublesome characters under your wings. This way they are controllable to an extent. Moreover when they shine, you glow too. Shastri understood this.

In his first Presidential tenure, Obama took his rival Hillary in his cabinet so that she does not create trouble outside. The nuance to note here is that he did not take her as an immediate subordinate but a level further away.

Empathy Towards Subordinates

(Circa 1962)

When Shastriji was the Home Minister, he was working late in his office with his Special Assistant in the South Block. While Shastriji sat in his chair, the official kept standing for a long time discussing the files with him as there was place only for one chair. After 10pm or so, Shastriji realized that the Special Assistant had kept standing for more than one hour. He was apologetic and said, "Why don't you sit down?" The Special Assistant said that there were only 3-4 files left and it would take only a few more minutes for the Minister to clear them. The Home Minister got up from his chair and said, "I too have been sitting for a long time and it would be a good idea to see the rest of my files while standing."

The Special Assistant was touched by the gesture of his

Minister and mentioned this to all his colleagues. During one of his tours, Shastriji was accompanied by the same Special Assistant. His accommodation arrangement was made at Raj Bhawan. On reaching his room Shastriji decided to walk into the Special Assistant's room to see if it was comfortable. Shastriji told the staff at Raj Bhawan, "Please don't mistake him for a PA (Personal Assistant), he is a senior IAS officer of UP cadre and should be looked after well." The Special Assistant was again touched by the extraordinary courtesy and consideration displayed by his boss.

Wisdom Window

Shastri understood the need to motivate employees to keep them happy in their jobs.

In his case, since it was a government setup, he could not provide much monetary incentive so by getting up and standing next to his Special Assistant, he provided motivational incentive – an egalitarian ethos between the superior and subordinate is also an incentive. Also with this gesture, he displayed civility.

Chairing a Meeting of the Congress Parliamentary Party (CPP)

(Circa 1963)

Morarji Desai was a senior colleague of Lal Bahadur Shastri. When Shastriji was the Home Minister, Morarji was the Finance Minister in Nehru's Cabinet. Nehruji had taken ill and an urgent meeting of the Congress Parliamentary Party had to be held. Since there was no Deputy Leader of the Congress Parliamentary Party (CPP) , the question arose about who would chair the meeting in the absence of Nehru. The practice of having a Deputy Leader of CPP was abandoned and a Deputy Leader each was nominated in Lok Sabha and Rajya Sabha for the purpose of House matters only.

Morarji Desai unexpectedly drove down to our house to meet my father. Shastriji was taken aback and enquired from him if there was something urgent. Morarji told him that he was keen to be seen as number two after Nehru and also told him that Jagjivan Ram also wanted the same. Jagjivan Ramji's claim was due to the fact that he was a Member of Nehru's first Cabinet after independence.

Shastriji said to Morarji how was it that he came to take his advice when he considered him as his political adversary. (Morarji would always tell people that the only person who would come in the way of his becoming Prime Minister after Nehru was Lal Bahadur Shastri). Morarji Desai said to Shastri

that he had come to him for advice as he believed that his intellectual honesty was unquestionable. He was sure that Lal Bahadur would give him the correct advice.

Shastriji did advise Morarji and asked him to reach the Parliament for the meeting half an hour before it would start. The meeting was being held in the Parliament House at 10 am and Shastriji suggested to Morarji to be there at 9.30 am. Thus, Morarji Desai reached Parliament at 9.30 am and occupied Nehru's chair. Jagjivan Ramji reached later but since Morarji Desai was already occupying Nehru's chair, he was allowed to chair the meeting.

Wisdom Window

Three very important indicators of establishing power protocol are Meeting, Greeting and Seating. Shastri understood this.

Meeting: Who has called the meeting, when is it happening and at whose convenience.

Greeting: Who addresses whom as what - Mr./Sir/First name.

Seating: Who takes the head chair.

Knowing the importance of seating Lal Bahadur told Morarji to be there at the venue half an hour before the meeting and occupy the head chair.

Aap Saath Chalna Pasand Karenge?

(Would you like to come along with me?)
(Circa 1964)

Whenever Shastriji wanted somebody to accompany him on his way to office or on his way to airport or even when he would go on a tour, he normally would say, "Aap saath chalna pasand karenge (would you like to come along)?" That was his polite way of letting the person know that he wanted to have a word with him on the way. But despite the gentleness in the phrasing, it was like a command written in stone as the incident below demonstrates.

In January 1964, Jawaharlal Nehru had taken ill in Bhubaneshwar and Shastriji who had resigned under Kamraj Plan was brought back into the Cabinet as minister without portfolio to assist the Prime Minister. Shastriji sent for his previous Special Assistant, Rajeshwar Prasad and asked him to rejoin him. When the officer said that he was already under orders of reversion to UP and was expecting his posting any day, Shastriji remarked, "We will see what can be done."

A few days later, Lal Bahadur Shastri was asked by Prime Minister Nehru to visit Srinagar. It was 25th of January, a very cold day in Delhi and Shastriji knew that Srinagar would be even colder. The problem was that the sacred relic of Hazratbal had disappeared and this had created lot of tension in the valley. It appeared as if Kashmir would be up in flames. The ailing Prime Minister was confident of Shastriji and that is why asked him to fly to Srinagar early next morning.

After getting instruction from Pandit Nehru, Shastriji rang up Rajeshwar Prasad with his favorite phrase, "Aap saath chalna pasand karenge (would you like to come along)?" Rajeshwar Prasad said that he was running high temperature and was in bed and that the doctors had advised him to guard against exposure to severe cold. Shastriji replied that the doctors were right but since this is an important mission he should carry enough woollens to protect himself from the severe cold of Kashmir. It was on the morning of 30th January 1964 that Lal Bahadur Shastri travelled to Srinagar for the historic visit which saw him resolving the Hazratbal crisis. During his stay in Srinagar, he made it a point to see that Rajeshwar Prasad was comfortable in every way. He even advised the local authorities on the menu that should be made available to his ailing Special Assistant.

Wisdom Window

Indian Civil Service, as bureaucracy was known then, was very strong and did not listen easily to politicians. Shastri was assertive but not aggressive.

His was an iron hand in a velvet glove. He set the agenda without rubbing the civil servant the wrong way and made sure that results were achieved. No reason or excuse that defeated or veered away from the purpose was entertained.

Pratap Singh Kairon

(Circa 1964)

When Lal Bahadur Shastri was the Home Minister in Nehru's Cabinet, there were certain allegations of misuse of office against the then Chief Minister (CM) of Punjab, Sardar Pratap Singh Kairon. Shastriji had felt at that time that the CM should quit on moral grounds. Shastriji mentioned this to Pt. Nehru who felt that Pratap Singh Kairon was a towering personality in Punjab and it would not be easy to find his replacement in the State and therefore was not very keen to disturb the situation. Nonetheless, he asked Shastriji to speak to Pratap Singh Kairon. Somehow Kairon was not inclined to resign and continued as Chief Minister of Punjab.

When Lal Bahadur Shastri became the Prime Minister on 9th June 1964, he sent for the Chief Minister of Punjab and sought his resignation. Kairon knew that it would be difficult to function without the support of the Prime Minister and thus resigned from his post. On the same day Lal Bahadur Shastri managed a smooth transition of leadership in Punjab by ensuring unanimous election of Ch. Ram Kishen as the new Chief Minister. All of this Shastriji accomplished within 30 days of his assuming office as Prime Minister.

Though Shastriji appeared to be soft spoken, he was actually a tough man. In this incident he showed how the Prime Minister's authority could be exercised by not only asking Pratap Singh Kairon to quit but also ensuring a unanimous election of a new leader.

There was a time when misuse of office by a Minister or a Chief Minister was taken very seriously and in almost all cases politicians holding these positions would have to go. It is ironical that today political leaders are not prepared to resign even when convicted by courts. The Supreme Court had to intervene by ruling that convicted elected representatives should be disqualified. The entire political class has taken offence on the ground that judiciary was encroaching upon their domain.

Wisdom Window

A great leader moves fast in the beginning of his tenure and makes some dramatic changes to create awe about himself. This is what Lal Bahadur did as he became the Prime Minister and made a powerful person like Kairon resign.

Morarji Opts Out of Shastri's Cabinet

(Circa 1964)

After Lal Bahadur Shastri was elected as leader of the Congress Parliamentary Party and was invited by the President to form the Government, he got busy with cabinet formation. By and large he retained the same ministers as in Nehru's Cabinet. Although Morarji Desai was not in Panditji's last cabinet, Shastriji invited him to be in his Government. Morarji agreed but wanted the No. 2 position in the cabinet and also the Home portfolio. Shastriji was reluctant to give Home portfolio because it was already held by another senior leader, Gulzari Lal Nanda. Shastriji explained his predicament to Morarji and said it would be difficult for him to convince Nandaji to leave the Home portfolio. Morarji finally agreed to accept the Ministry of Food and Agriculture with No.2 position. Shastriji agreed to this but suddenly Gulzari Lal Nanda declined to give up the No. 2 position in the cabinet at the instance of some senior Congress leaders. He said he would rather give up the Home portfolio but not the position.

Lal Bahadur Shastri requested Morarji Desai to come over to his residence and conveyed Gulzari Lal Nanda's stance. He said, "Nandaji says that since he is the interim Prime Minister after Nehru's death, he should be given the No. 2 position in the cabinet." Morarji was upset and opted out telling Shastriji, "Let Gulzari Lal take both, the Home portfolio and the No.2

position. The need of the hour is that the party should remain united." Morarji left Shastriji's residence and the matter ended there.

Lal Bahadur Shastri was keen to have Morarji Desari in his Cabinet but perhaps was not willing to upset other senior leaders including Gulzari Lal Nanda. He had sensed that Nanda changed his mind at the behest of some senior colleagues. He also agreed with Morarji that there was no point in precipitating matters so soon after Pt. Jawaharlal Nehru's death. Already, there was a big vacuum in the party and in the country after Nehru's death.

Wisdom Window

A leader sometimes needs to recognize the talents of an adversary as well as appreciate the fact that certain adversaries need to be kept in close proximity rather than at a distance. This is why perhaps Shastri offered Morarji the No. 2 position in his cabinet.

Knowing also that such a move could create rifts (from his earlier experience of seeing the friction between Jawahar Lal Nehru and his No. 2 Ballabh Pant who was himself a strong personality), he offered Morarji No. 2 position but not the Home Portfolio as Home had control of Police as well as Intelligence. Devoid of the powerful Home portfolio, the No. 2 position was hardly appealing.

T.T. Krishnamachari

(Circa 1965)

When T.T. Krishnamachari was the Finance Minister in Lal Bahadur Shastri's cabinet, there were some allegations of misuse of power. TTK, as he was popularly known, expected the Prime Minister to defend him on the floor of the House to which Shastriji did not agree. TTK was upset and offered his resignation to Shastriji which he accepted with regret. On the same day he appointed Sachindra Choudhury as his new Finance Minister. I remember that my father spoke to the then Congress President Shri Kamraj, over the telephone who was in Chennai (then Madras) and informed him that he had accepted TTK's resignation and appointed Sachindra Choudhury as the new Finance Minister. My brother-in-law, Shri Kaushal Kumar was also there in the room and wondered whether the Congress President would be upset with Shastriji for not having consulted with him before taking such a major decision. Shastriji said to him softly but firmly, "Who should or should not be in his Cabinet was the prerogative of the Prime Minister and he would not want this prerogative to be diluted in any way." He further said, "Pt. Nehru gave power and authority to the office of Prime Minister which I will ensure does not get eroded."

Wisdom Window

A good leader is consultative when it comes to policy matters. However when it comes to matters of principle, he is singularly definitive and takes firm decisions without needing anybody's endorsement.

Relations with Indira Gandhi

(Circa 1946 - 1966)

Lal Bahadur Shastri's relations with Indira Gandhi remained cordial all along. They had established a good working rapport from his early political career until he passed away as India's Prime Minister. They both consulted with each other quite often over different issues concerning the party and the country. When Indira Gandhi was appointed as the President of the Indian National Congress, Shastriji was the Union Minister for Transport and Communication and later Minister for Commerce and Industry.

In 1963, the party felt that some senior Cabinet Ministers and Chief Ministers should quit the Government to take up organizational responsibilities. Lal Bahadur Shastri was the Home Minister and was the first to resign under the Kamraj Plan. Others followed suit; leaders like Morarji Desai and Jagjivan Ram at the Centre and Biju Patnaik and C.B. Gupta in Orissa and UP. Six months later when Shastriji was absorbed back into the Cabinet by Pt. Nehru as Minister without portfolio, it had the backing of Indira Gandhi. After Panditji's death, Shastri along with Kamraj had requested Indiraji to accept the responsibility of Prime Minister but she politely declined and cited her father's death as the reason.

When Lal Bahadur Shastri succeeded Jawaharlal Nehru

and was in the process of forming his Cabinet, he was keen to have Indira Gandhi in his Cabinet and requested her for consent. Initially, Indiraji was reluctant and wanted to be left alone for some time after her father's death. But when Shastriji insisted that she would be a source of strength to him in the government, she agreed on condition that she would accept a light portfolio like Information and Broadcasting. This portfolio at that time was not very pressurising. Thus, Indiraji was sworn in as Union Minister in Shastriji's cabinet at No. 4 position after Gulzari Lal Nanda and T.T. Krishnamachari.

After Shastriji's death, Indira Gandhi took over as Prime Minister and allotted a government bungalow to my mother Lalita Shastri and the family, since we did not have a house to live in anywhere in India. My father died penniless and Indiraji was aware of this. She even sanctioned a pension of Rs. 1000/- per month to my mother and offered to waive off the loan which Shastriji had taken to buy a car.

Indira Gandhi had so much of regard for Shastriji that she would often enquire from my mother if all was well with the family. She gave Lok Sabha ticket to my elder brother Hari Shastri and UP Assembly ticket to my younger brother Sunil Shastri as long as she was alive. She even made Sunil a Minister in UP at the young age of 30. My father always used to say that Indira Gandhi was a very compassionate person and I absolutely agree that no politician can match her compassion and greatness even today.

Wisdom Window

A great leader carries his relationships right to the grave. Shastri fostered his relationships in such a way that they lasted even after he was no more. He left behind a wealth of goodwill and a legacy of admiration.

The Witty Shastri

(Circa 1964 - 1966)

When Shastriji was elected leader of the Congress Parliamentary Party and was Prime Minister designate, he was yet to take oath of office. After his election, he was addressing a press conference at his residence. One correspondent asked him whether he would have a Deputy Prime Minister. Shastriji replied that he was not yet the Prime Minister so where was the question of having a Deputy Prime Minister! The correspondents burst into laughter.

There was another remark from a correspondent that why didn't he tell his sons to wear simple khadi clothes like him instead of the fashionable trousers and shirts. Shastriji said that his father was a poor school teacher whereas their father was India's Prime Minister !

During the Indo-Pak war, Zulfikar Ali Bhutto, the then Foreign Minister of Pakistan, had said that they would stroll down to Delhi to have dinner there. Shastriji when asked about it retorted that though Delhi is far but by tomorrow our armed forces will stroll up to Lahore.

When Lal Bahadur Shastri was to leave for his ill-fated trip to Tashkent on January 3, 1966, one correspondent at the airport jocularly asked him, would he not suffer from an inferiority complex talking to Ayub Khan a much taller person than him. Shastriji smilingly said, "Not at all. I would raise my head to speak to him whereas he would have to bend down!"

Wisdom Window

Sometimes the questions media asks are difficult to answer and provocative in nature. Seasoned politicians and statesmen often use humour to either deflect the issue or handle it obliquely. In the ensuing laughter, most people remember the joke and forget the issue.

Using humour is also a sign of mental agility and lateral thinking.

Affable Personality

(Circa 1965)

A Member of Parliament from the opposing Swatantra Party, Shri Mahida Narendra Singh was very upset with Shastriji. It so happened that Shastriji as Prime Minister visited Anand in Gujarat which happened to be the constituency of Mahida Narendra Singh. The Prime Minister's office did not inform the MP about the Prime Minister's visit to his constituency. Shri Singh, who was also General Secretary of the Swatantra Party, advised his workers not to accord any reception to the Prime Minister on his arrival at Anand.

Later in the day, when Shastriji got to learn about the lapse on the part of his office, he immediately decided to visit him at his residence and regretted the lapse. Mahida Narendra Singh was so touched by Shastriji's gesture that he later left the Swatantra Party and rejoined the Congress.

Wisdom Window

Lal Bahadur Shastri was an organization builder. When he realized that he had inadvertently bypassed his colleague from Anand he quickly corrected his mistake, and through his personal touch got the talented resource back in his team.

Saying 'No' Elegantly

(Circa 1964)

Dr. Shankar Dayal Sharma, former President of India, once told me an anecdote about Shastriji. Shankar Dayal Sharma was a senior leader of the Congress Party in Madhya Pradesh and was pretty close to Shastriji. He was looking for an opportunity to come to central politics. Lal Bahadur Shastri became the Prime Minister in 1964. Dr. Sharma mustered some courage and conveyed to him his desire of coming to central politics in Delhi.

Shastriji needed him to continue in Madhya Pradesh for political reasons. He therefore paused for a while and said, "Although you will be an asset to me in Delhi, who will be my man in Madhya Pradesh? I need someone like you to look after my work in the State for some more time." Shankar Dayal Sharma had nothing to say after that and was happy continuing in Madhya Pradesh politics as Shastriji's confidante.

Wisdom Window

Lal Bahadur refused Shankar Dayal in such a tactful and motivational manner that Shankar Dayal proudly repeated this conversation to whoever he met. Shastri gave him pride in refusal and made him see value in a way he wasn't seeing. The 'NO' transformed into a 'Badge of Honour'.

Effective leaders apply this art of tactfully saying 'No' without hurting the subordinate's pride and morale.

Never Pulling Ranks

(Circa 1965)

After finishing school, I had gone to seek admission at St. Stephen's College in the year 1965 for my undergraduate degree. My father was the Prime Minister then. I submitted the form duly filled in and delivered it at the reception counter. I had written my name as Anil Kumar, father's name as L.B. Shastri, his occupation as government service and address 10, Janpath. Just before my turn came for the interview, one Mr. Robert from the office called me to enquire whether I lived at 10 Janpath which was then the Prime Minister's house. I said 'yes' and then he asked what my father did for a living. Our family upbringing had made us so humble and modest that all I could say was that he was holding a government position as mentioned in my form. When Mr. Robert persisted with me to know his designation, I replied that he was Prime Minister of India. I could see that he was in a state of shock for a moment.

He took me aside and went in the Principal's room to perhaps inform the Principal. One faculty member came out and said hello to me and asked me to wait and promised to free me early from the interview.

In the evening when I reached home and mentioned about this to Shastriji, he said the first part of you waiting in the queue was good but somehow he didn't like the second part where I was given a preferrential treatment just because of my background.

Wisdom Window

On probing Anil Shastri further on this episode, I came to know that his father was perturbed by the fact that Anil was taken to the Principal's office by the person who was supposed to be attending to the queue of waiting students. The students therefore had to wait for an extra 20 to 30 minutes while the office was showering attention on Anil, and this pained Shastri.

A similar spirit is resonated in Mahatama Gandhi's favourite Hindi bhajan:
'Vaishnav Jan Tene Kahiye Peer Parayee Jane Re'
(in English it means: The truly spiritual man is one who understands the pain of others.)

Interacting with Girls

(Circa 1965)

At 17 years of age, I got admission at St. Stephen's College to study Economic (Honours). As a normal teenager, I had friends, both boys and girls, in the college as well as at University. One afternoon after college, a few girls came to meet me at my residence. My father who was then the Prime Minister was about to arrive for lunch from office around the same time. I felt shy to be seen with girls so decided to hide. Subsequently I sent a message at the gate that I wasn't home.

As Shastriji was entering the house, he noticed 3-4 girls waiting at the gate. When he was told that they had come to meet me, he politely asked them to come in. On getting to know that I was very much in the house, he sent for me. I could see that he wasn't happy with the way I treated my guests who had come to meet me. When asked, I told him that I was shy and thought that he might not like my meeting girls. He responded with a little firmness that

I should not jump to conclusions. Why would he mind my meeting girls of my age? He asked me to get them in and look after them well. My father's advice was that for generations, guests in India were treated with respect and dignity and therefore they should be given due regard by me. Hospitality, he said, was the key to Indian culture. I met my friends immediately and apologised to them for having lied that I was not at home and for having made them wait at the gate.

Wisdom Window

Shastri recognised the natural nature of opposite sex relationships. He did not ignore or brush them under the carpet.

In India, sex is a taboo and we repress our natural feelings for the opposite sex in public. These feelings then come out with many times the force in private. No wonder our population grows unbridled and sex-related crimes are rampant.

Treating opposite sex friendships normally helps healthy interaction.

Values Vital for a Healthy Society

A healthy democracy requires a decent society; it requires that we are honorable, generous, tolerant and respectful.

- Charles W Pickering

Lal Bahadur Shastri believed in the greater good of mankind. He saw himself as an enabler, a catalyst who did his utmost to propel the country forward. He was progressive and liberal.

Even when tough decisions had to be made, he always focused on the impact it would have on Indians at large.

Caste Connotations

(Circa 1916)

Lal Bahadur Shastri noticed that he was registered in school as Lal Bahadur Varma when he was in Class VI in the school at Moghalsarai. Though Shastriji was just a 12 year old boy at that time, he expressed his desire to his mother and family members to delete his surname from school record as he was against the caste system.

Munshi Darbari Lal, who was Shastriji's maternal grandfather, did not raise any objection. His son Bindeshwari Prasad, who also had no surname, favoured the idea of Lal Bahadur. They all came together and applied to the headmaster for the deletion of the surname 'Varma' in Lal Bahadur's school record. Though the headmaster himself was

a 'Varma' i.e. Basant Lal Varma, he was not annoyed at the proposal and approved it. Lal Bahadur Varma was thereafter known as just Lal Bahadur. 'Shastri' was added to his name in 1925, when he acquired the degree of 'Shastri' (one who knows the Shastras) from the Kashi Vidyapeeth in Varanasi.

Wisdom Window

Lal Bahadur, even at a young age was against fragmentation of the society on the basis of caste. That's why he wished to have his surname removed from his name as it was the surname which carries the caste identity.

Family v/s Country

(Circa 1940)

Once when Shastriji was in jail, my elder sister, Manju, fell seriously ill. According to jail rules, Shastriji could be released on parole after signing a declaration that he would not engage in any political activity during that period. Shastriji said that it was not proper for a freedom fighter to sign any such declaration and hence the jail superintendent, who had high regard for Shastriji and trusted him a lot, allowed him to leave the jail on parole for fifteen days without signing the declaration. Unfortunately, when Shastriji reached home, my sister passed away. He performed the last rites and immediately went back to jail, without utilizing the fifteen days' parole granted to him.

On another occasion, my eldest brother Hari Krishan, who was four years old at that time, was suffering with typhoid. He was running high fever and his condition was not improving.

Shastriji was allowed a parole on this occasion, again without any conditions. He went home and took care of his ailing son but unfortunately his condition became worse. When the parole period was about to end, the jail superintendent told Shastriji that the parole could be extended but he had to sign an undertaking that he would not engage in any political activity. Though Hari Krishan wanted his father by his side, Lal Bahadur Shastri did not succumb to emotions and declined this conditional offer and went back to jail on time.

Wisdom Window

It was Shastri's spirit of defiance against the British rule because of which he did not sign the parole paper or tow the line. Not signing was his way of voicing that the British occupation of India was unlawful and they could not make him sign the so called legal paper. He did not want to give up his right to campaign against them and demand their ouster.

There were tears in his eyes for his children but resolute defiance in his march against British Imperialism.

Dreams of Serving the Nation

(Circa 1945)

Way back in 1945, Lal Bahadur Shastri had gone with a friend to watch the proceedings of the Parliament. This was before independence and therefore the Treasury Benches were occupied by the British whereas the Opposition Benches were occupied by Congress stalwarts like Jawaharlal Nehru, Sardar Vallabh Bhai Patel, Pandit Govind Ballabh Pant, Dr. Rajendra Prasad and many more. The debate was in full swing and the opposition leaders were blasting the Government and making their life miserable. The debate was interesting for young Shastri who was greatly impressed with the debating skills of our leaders in the opposition.

He shared his wish with his friend that one day he would also like to be a member of that august house. The friend looked at him, smiled and sarcastically said that he should never dream something which was impossible to achieve. Lal Bahadur Shastri was hurt but kept quiet.

Nineteen years later in

1964, Shastriji became India's Prime Minister succeeding Jawaharlal Nehru. As Prime Minister, he was the leader of the House. It was ironical for his friend watching him from the public gallery of Parliament House. Shastriji looked at him and smiled.

In the evening after coming home, my father narrated the story to us. I asked him why he had not reminded his friend about what he had said to him many years ago. My father put his hand on my shoulder and said, "What would be the difference between me and my friend then? He must have realized by now that what he had said to me was inappropriate."

Wisdom Window

When Anil asked Shastriji as to why he did not remind his friend about what he had said years ago, Shastri said that he did not do so because he felt his friend must already be regretting saying that and also by reminding him he would have disclosed the fact that he remembered that incident.

Through his achievement, he had convincingly won the argument and knew that after defeating somebody decisively, you should allow him to retreat gracefully and not humiliate him further.

Instead of creating further rift, he invited his friend to his cabinet. Through such gestures, yesterday's rivals can be future allies for a bigger war.

Regard for Sincere and Committed Employees

(Circa 1950 - 1954)

Kanhaiya Lal, Lal Bahadur Shastri's nephew (elder sister's son) was employed with the Indian Railways as an engine driver. When Shastriji became the Railway Minister and people got to know his relationship with Kanhaiya Lal, they were surprised. It so happened that Shastriji was once travelling in a train as the Railway Minister and he got to learn that his nephew was driving the engine. He sent for him immediately at the next station. Kanhaiya Lal sent a message back to Shastriji saying, "If you are calling me in your capacity as a Minister, I will obey your orders but if you want to meet your nephew, I do not wish to leave the engine unattended."

There was another incident when Lal Bahadur Shastri was stopped by a police constable at a railway station when he was UP's Home Minister. The constable said, "I will not allow you to go ahead since our Home Minister has already arrived by the same train and I have to make way for him." Immediately officials came running and scolded the constable. Shastriji asked them not to do so and rather complimented the constable for doing his duty properly. In fact he asked him if he would like to be part of his security staff to which the constable happily agreed. This was Lal Bahadur Shastri's way of appreciating and rewarding those who were perfect in performing their duties.

Wisdom Window

Shastri recognized one's deepest affiliation should be to his duty rather than to powers that be. For him, duty was the stern daughter of the Voice of God and he not only showed utmost commitment to his duties, he admired people who could put duty above everything else. That's the reason he admired his nephew even when he could not come to meet him. He similarly appreciates the constable who stopped him in his tracks.

Shastri's ego was so reined in that he did not take affront from his nephew who admissibly flouted the command of the Railway Minister to fulfil his duty or from the constable who failed to recognize his Home Minister. For him, duty was higher than any office in the land.

Against Untouchability

(Circa 1952)

In April 1952, Shastriji was included by Pt. Nehru as India's Railway Minister. I was, of course, too young to remember these important events of that time. However, there is one incident which impacted me and I remember it even today.

During his constituency tours, Shastriji would visit the homes of Congress workers. This was common practice in those days. Once he was invited for lunch by an upper caste family in a village. Shastriji noticed that a few plates had been segregated for serving food to the Dalit workers. He was aware of the caste discrimination which persisted in the society. He could not accept this and asked the host to serve him food in one of those plates meant for the Dalits. The host pleaded with him not to do so as there were different plates meant for the upper castes. Shastriji said that if he wanted

him to eat lunch in his house, he would have to serve him food in the plates meant for the Dalit community, otherwise he would not eat at all. The host had to relent and he removed all those plates which were kept aside for the Dalit workers. And thus, everybody ate in the same type of plates without any discrimination.

Wisdom Window

*Mahatama Gandhi and Lal Bahadur Shastri understood that caste is the social violence of a militarily non-violent nation.**

They did their best to correct this malaise in whichever way the situation demanded.

**Indians were a glorious race but as per Hutton and sociologists like him, they were reluctant to fight against the invaders militarily. So they chose the easier option by bringing in the concept of caste system and declared all the invading tribes as low caste, and neither associated with them nor educated them.*

Handling Unresponsive Officials

(Circa 1952 – 1966)

Lal Bahadur Shastri during his ministerial assignments and later on as Prime Minister would come across certain officials who were not receptive to people's needs and aspirations. Shastriji felt that since they were not familiar with the grass root problems of the common man, they were not able to comprehend and address their grievances. He would do his best to counsel the officials and would give them the opportunity to learn and improve. But when he found out that a particular officer was not mending his ways, he would shift him to another assignment. Of course, Shastriji would ensure that the new assignment would not involve public dealing. While transferring the officer, he would also see to it that the new job does not demotivate him.

Wisdom Window

One of the most desired man management abilities is the ability to match the man to the job. And Shastri had this ability and used it wisely, while all the time ensuring the changes he effected did not cause demotivation.

Accessible to All People

(Circa 1953)

When Lal Bahadur Shastri was the Railway Minister, railway guards used to hold kerosene lanterns to give green or red signal to the drivers of the trains. At that time, there used to be a guard who was considered very honest. His name was Shri Shankar Sahai Srivastava. On the other hand many of his colleagues drew much more kerosene oil from the store than required and use it in their homes, and they also stole coal meant for railway engines. Shankar Sahai detested all these malpractices; as a result he was an eyesore for his colleagues and seniors and often got harassed in the form of transfers and suspensions.

During the 1953 Kumbh Mela in Allahabad, Shastriji's mother and Shankar Sahai's mother happened to be occupying the same tent. After brief introductions, when guard Srivastava's mother came to know that she was Railway Minster's mother, she expressed the problems he son was facing due to his honesty. He happened to be under suspension at that time. When Shastriji came to meet his mother in her tent and offered respect to all the senior women present in the tent, he enquired about their well-being. Shastriji's mother told him about guard Srivastava's plight. Lal Bahadur Shastri was deeply moved and immediately gave his personal telephone number to guard Srivastava's mother and told her that her son should call him when he (Shastriji) returned to Delhi. He assured to help him. As soon as he reached Delhi, he called for the relevant records and after checking, took action to withdraw Shri Srivastava's suspension.

Wisdom Window

Shastri showed kindness in assuring help to a stranger coming from a very different strata of society. He also showed judiciousness by not promising results unless all investigation was conducted. He first did the due diligence by checking all records and only when satisfied took necessary action.

General Elections

(Circa 1957)

In the general elections of 1957, Shastriji was in charge of the disbursement of Congress party funds. Although there were several offers, he abstained from seeking an amount in excess of the sum allotted to other Congress candidates for his own election. Even though he was short of electoral funds, he chose to keep it that way.

It was an open secret that greater honours and more important offices would be conferred on him after the elections. Many would have been eager to extend a helping hand to him. However, he turned his eyes away from them.

Wisdom Window

Shastri was a symbol of scrupulousness and he believed in fairness. He did not want more than what was being given to others. He did not want any money from business houses.

He wanted to win playing by the rules. He rationalized that for the end to be good, the means should be good too. Fortune favoured him and he won the elections despite limited means.

Praying to God in 30 Seconds

(Circa 1959)

Once, when I was a small kid, I asked my father if he offered prayers to God or performed his regular 'pooja' like my mother? He said much that he would like to do so, could not find time for regular 'pooja'. However, he said that he did pray to God early morning just for 30 seconds. It was quite intriguing to me what could it be that he prayed for only 30 seconds. I asked him and he replied his prayer quite simply was, "Nothing should I say or do during the day which would hurt somebody's feelings."

Wisdom Window

Shastri's prayer is also a digestive for his power. This great man understood that such supreme power, as was vested in him, needs restraint. Therefore he asked God every day to rein him in.

Akali Agitation - Fast unto Death

(Circa 1962)

When Shastriji was Home Minister, Master Tara Singh, a senior and renowned Akali leader in Punjab decided to go on a hunger strike to demand for a Punjabi Suba. He had gone on fast unto death and this was causing lot of anxious moments in government circles as everyone was aware of the consequences if Master Tara Singh died.

Shastriji was sitting in his chamber in the South Block discussing the matter with his senior officials. One officer suggested, "Surely we can arrange for him to be fed even against his will." Shastriji reacted sharply and it was the first time that the officials saw him very angry. He said, "What the British did not do to Gandhiji and the rest of us during the freedom struggle, you want us to do after Independence. They were also aware of the consequences if Gandhiji had died during any of his numerous

fasts, but never did they do him the indignity of trying to force-feed him. If a man is prepared to make the supreme sacrifice of his life for a cause he holds dear, who are we to trample on human dignity and inflict this sort of insult upon him?"

Shastriji decided to travel to Punjab for negotiations with Master Tara Singh. They talked and talked for hours together. Nobody aided either side in the discussions. After many hours late in the night, he came out smilingly from Master Tara Singh's room and announced to the bewilderment of media and officials that the Akali leader had agreed to give up his fast. However, Master Tara Singh told Shastriji that he will be doing penance in the Golden Temple in the form of cleaning shoes and washing used utensils in the Gurudwara.

Wisdom Window

This anecdote demonstrates that the dignity of your opponent should be kept intact. One should not run roughshod over your opponents even when he has the power to do so.

Another self-imposed control on Shastri's power was his concern for the dignity of the opponent. His wisdom and tenacity told him what currently appeared never-ending would eventually get resolved and come to an end.

Whenever you are at cross-purposes with someone, consider

all options. Force is not the best option even if you are much more powerful than your opponent. Even if you make your opponent genuflect with a brute show of force, you can't make him forget the humiliation of his defeat. Its memories will come to haunt him and brew resentment in him. He may plot revenge, or at least gloat when you fall.

In 1947, Lal Bahadur became the Minister of Police and Transport in Shri Pant's Ministry. Usually the minister in charge of the Police Department did not remain popular for long, but this wasn't the case with Shastri. He never allowed the police to resort to lathi charge and firing. He ordered use of water jets instead of lathis to disperse unruly crowds. Though there were many strikes in Uttar Pradesh when he was in office, there was not a single occasion when people shouted slogans against him.

Not only was the dignity of the individual but the quantum of pain inflicted on the wrong doer was important to him.

Shastri did not believe in using a sledgehammer to nail a drawing pin. That is why he deployed water jets instead of lathi charge.

Kashmir Issue

(Circa 1964)

It was the month of January 1964, when the Hazratbal sacred relic consisting of the hair of the Prophet went missing from the Hazratbal Shrine. This gave rise to a passionate outcry in the Kashmir valley. Shastriji was immediately summoned by Prime Minister Nehru. He was told to proceed to Srinagar to see that the matter was resolved to the satisfaction of all.

It was bitterly cold in Srinagar and Pandit Nehru gave his warm overcoat to Shastriji to protect him from the Kashmir winter. Shastriji landed in Srinagar and met several people. The most influential people at that time were Maulana Masoodi of the National Conference and Mirwaiz Maulvi Farooq. These were the people who needed to be shown the relic to convince them that it was found and was genuine. Shastriji was fully aware of the risk involved which had already been highlighted to him by the Home Secretary and the Director, Intelligence Bureau (IB).

Later in the day, he came to know from one of his team members that the Home Secretary and the Director, IB were of the opinion that if Shastriji wished to preserve his reputation for sorting out difficult problems, it would be advisable for him to go back to Delhi by the first available plane. He kept quiet.

The next day, he called the Home Secretary and the Director(IB) for a meeting and told them that as a result of his talks with the local leaders, he was convinced that showing (Deedaar in Urdu) of the relic was essential. However Shastriji assured the Home Secretary and the Director, that if they were apprehensive of the decision, he would make sure they would not be held responsible if anything went wrong and would make the arrangements with the help of the younger officers. In that case, he would advise them to go back to Delhi by the first available plane.

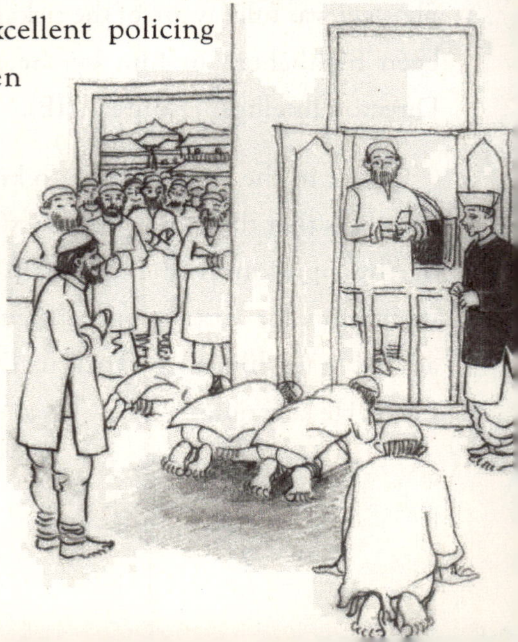

Shri Rajeshwar Prasad, IAS who was Private Secretary to Shastriji at that time and had accompanied him to Srinagar has stated in his biography on Shastriji that, "The occasion of the 'Deedar' in the Hazartbal Shrine next afternoon was one fraught with tension and anxiety. It was a cold, cloudy afternoon with snow all around, and the Mosque on the banks of the Dal Lake as well as the surrounding areas were jam-packed with people. Excellent policing arrangements had been made, but the police was very much in the background. Shastriji was there along with Maulana Masoodi and the other leaders. It was a tense moment, because if the recovered relic was not accepted as genuine, bloodshed was inevitable. But the moment the relic was put on display, Maulana Masoodi and others took a look at it, and then prostrated themselves on the floor before it.

Those standing behind, and in the courtyard could hardly see the relic, but their leaders' reverence was sufficient for them and they all prostrated on the cold ground with cries of joy and devotion. What had been a period of nerve-tingling suspense became an occasion of rejoicing and celebration. The Home Secretary and the Director (IB), with broad smiles on their faces after many a long day, paid tribute to Shastriji's sagacity, when they saw him off at the airport later that evening."

Wisdom Window

Shastri made his calculated moves very much like the great statesman Chanakya.

He first unsettled the Home secretary and Director (IB) by telling them politely that they were free to leave, that they would not be held responsible in case of a mishap and he would manage without them.

He then instilled fear and insecurity in them further by suggesting offering their place to their juniors.

Like any brave warrior, he led from the front. No hurdle could dampen his enthusiasm. He taught how to take the bull by its horns.

Prisoner of Indecision

(Circa 1964)

Smt.Vijay Laxmi Pandit was Member of Parliament when Lal Bahadur Shastri was the Prime Minister. She got elected from Phulpur constituency in district Allahabad after a vacancy was necessitated by the death of Pt. Nehru. She was a forthright and straight-forward political leader and would say what she believed was right.

Since Lal Bahadur Shastri succeeded a towering personality, he obviously was seen as a weak Prime Minister in his stature as compared to Panditji. Shastriji himself admitted this by saying that his greatest handicap was that he was a successor to Jawaharlal Nehru. Vijay Laxmi Pandit, in one of her outbursts on government functioning, referred to Shastriji as 'a prisoner of indecision'. Shastriji was hurt and told her that since he was the duly elected leader of the party, she will have to bear with him.

It was a matter of time when Lal Bahadur Shastri's leadership qualities during the Indo-Pak war were noticed by all. His decisiveness in ordering the armed forces to retaliate with full force by opening up new fronts including Lahore not only surprised his colleagues and friends but also the armed forces. His firmness was demonstrated in ample measure in his speeches whenever he would refer to Pakistan during war time. The Indian armed forces were a motivated lot under his leadership. Vijay Laxmi Pandit was greatly impressed with the leadership that Lal Bahadur Shastri provided to the country during the 22 day war with Pakistan. She changed her opinion about him and told a correspondent from the Indian Express that, "It was a serious underestimation of a leader of outstanding and exceptional caliber." Shastriji on reading this, personally went to her house to thank her.

Wisdom Window

Shastri was not the type to react to every aspersion cast on him. He did not allow his relationship with Vijaylaxmi to sour even though he knew she did not approve of him as a leader. He was comfortable with himself as he was aware of his own capabilities and leadership qualities which he had had ample chance to realize while he was holding various ministerial portfolios.

Therefore rather than actively clearing the misconception voiced by Vijaylaxmi, he waited and in due course, she herself took back her words.

War against Pakistan

(Circa 1965)

It was the 31st of August 1965 when Shastriji was surprisingly having an early dinner. Around 8 pm, his Personal Assistant informed him that the three Chiefs of the Armed Forces wanted to see him. He immediately asked him to call them to the Prime Minister's house. Within a few minutes, the Chief of Air Staff, the Chief of Army and the Chief of Naval Staff turned up at 10 Janpath which was then Shastriji's residence.

Shastriji left the dining room to meet them in the office. Within 7 minutes he was back with us and continued with his dinner. We were wondering what had happened that the Chiefs had suddenly come to see him. When requested to tell us what transpired in the meeting, all he said was, "Be prepared for a war." He further elaborated that the Pakistan army had crossed the international border in the Chamb sector and if not stopped immediately, would cut off Jammu & Kashmir from the rest of the country. The only way to stop them was to open up new fronts to dilute their concentration in the Chamb sector. Shastriji instantly gave the go-ahead signal to the Chiefs and asked them to ensure that Lahore was also included.

Within few days, our army crossed the international border near Amritsar and started marching towards Lahore. General Ayub Khan who was the President of Pakistan instructed his army to protect Lahore from being captured by the Indians. And thus, the Pakistan army's concentration shifted from Chamb to save Lahore. Lal Bahadur Shastri had asked the Air Force to attack Pakistan through the air as well. This was the first time after independence that the Indian Air Force went into action and also the first time the Indian Army crossed the international border. The war lasted for 22 days and Indian Armed Forces captured some vantage points in the Pakistan territory.

Chief of Air Staff then was Air Marshal Arjan Singh who is now Marshal of the Air Force. He says that the country could not have had a better Prime Minister in war than Lal Bahadur Shastri. He further says that the promptness with which Shastriji gave the go-ahead signal to the armed forces could have come only from a brave, decisive and a firm leader.

Wisdom Window

However brilliant an action, it should not be esteemed great unless the result of a great motive.

- Francois La Rochefoucauld.

Though Shastri was seeped in the tradition of non-violence, and in not initiating violence, he demonstrated real politic in this instance.

After Chanakya, he was among the few Indian leaders who gave pride and honour to the Indian people. While other leaders talked of non-violence when action was required, he understood that this was the time of action. To counter the attack on Kashmir, he attacked Lahore and dispersed the Pakistani army.

Standing Tall

(Circa 1964)

Before the advent of television, a fortnightly news roundup used to be shown through newsreels in cinema halls across the country. This was perhaps mandatory. I remember that when Shastriji became Prime Minister, the audience in cinema halls would laugh on seeing him in the newsreels because he was not a tall, statuesque person like Nehru. I was in the last year of school at that time and would feel hurt and embarrassed over people laughing at my father. As we know, he succeeded Jawaharlal Nehru, a towering personality. His short stature was perhaps a matter of ridicule for the audience at that time.

This went on until the Indo-Pak war broke on 1st September 1965. The leadership that Lal Bahadur Shastri provided to the nation during the 22 day war period was remarkable. He suddenly earned respect from every corner of the country. His morale boosting speeches inspired the nation. There was a new sense of confidence and vigour amongst the people. The Indian armed forces felt elated over the fact that they had for the first time after independence crossed the international border and had reached the doorsteps of Lahore. It was after a long time in India's history that the battle was fought on enemy soil and this achievement was largely attributed to the leadership which Lal Bahadur Shastri provided at that time.

In an interview with a TV channel, Air Force Marshal Arjan Singh (the then Chief of Air Staff) said that there could not have been a better Prime Minister during the war time in 1965 than Lal Bahadur Shastri. Newspaper reports at that time had said that Shastriji, though underestimated initially, proved to be a leader of outstanding and exceptional calibre.

Post war, the scenario in the cinema halls in 1965 had changed. The same audience would clap and applause the moment they would see their Prime Minister on the screen. I felt so happy and shared my joy with my father. All he said was, "Great battles are won only if one has the will to fight. People admire the brave and not the meek."

Wisdom Window

The public tends to stereotype leaders.

Given Nehru's personality, a leader had to be tall, bold, impressive and a great speaker. Lal Bahadur was a complete contrast - short, quiet and an average speaker. So he did not fit the public's blueprint of a leader. They found him wanting as a leader but this did not perturb Shastri. He did not let these opinions trouble him, and through his bold action during war with Pakistan went on to create an image of himself bigger than any other Indian leader for some time to come.

Evidently, it is not about the height but the stature one achieves that matters.

A Credible Leader

(Circa 1965)

During the Indo-Pak war in September 1965, there was acute food shortage in the country and the problem was aggravated by the threat from President Lindon B. Johnson of the United States to stop wheat supplies to India. India used to import wheat from America under PL 480 which meant the payment could be made in Indian rupees instead of dollars. The US President tried to arm-twist India to declare cease-fire immediately. Perhaps, the American President mistook Shastri's stature as his weakness and thought his threat would work. In response, Prime Minister Lal Bahadur Shastri appealed to the nation to miss one meal a week. He suggested Mondays for this purpose.

The whole country knows even now, many decades after his death that Shastriji was a man of self-respect and would not, under any circumstances, have compromised with the dignity and honour of the Indian people. He preferred to remain hungry rather than going to America with a begging bowl. Shastriji countered the threat of America by appealing to the people of India to miss a meal on Monday evenings. There was instant response from the people of our country who began fasting on each Monday evening to thwart the pressure tactics of Lindon Johnson. Standing by his principles, Shastriji did not visit the United States even though he visited Canada as Prime Minister.

This trait was reflected in his childhood incident as well - when he would refuse the favour of the boatman and would rather swim across the mighty Ganges in Varanasi when he didn't have money to pay for the boat ride.

I would also like to mention here that before appealing to the nation to miss a meal, Prime Minister Shastri asked my mother Lalita Shastri not to cook food one evening. He told my mother that before I ask the people not to eat, I would like to know whether my children could remain hungry. It was only after he was satisfied that none of us had a problem skipping a meal, did he ask the countrymen to fast. Perhaps, it was his credibility which convinced the people of India that if their Prime Minister was appealing to them not to eat, he and his family were also doing the same. It is unfortunate that today there is no such credibility of people in public life in the eyes of our countrymen.

Wisdom Window

This anecdote reveals two traits of Shastri's character, self-respect and tenacity. It was his self-respect that made him swim rather than take the boat. It was the same self-respect which made him refuse to go to the US with a begging bowl.

It was his tenacity that helped him take on the mighty Ganges, and stay on course. By the same principle, he did not visit the most powerful country in the world even though he was visiting its neighbour, Canada.

Shastri was not just a leader who led from the front but also took people along with him. Before he could ask people to wear an uncomfortable shoe, he would walk in it to see how it felt. Only when he was convinced that he and his family could bear the discomfort of fasting did he go public with his demand. That is why he always got a heart-felt and overwhelming response.

Jai Jawan Jai Kisan

(1965)

In the midst of Indo-Pak war in September 1965 Lal Bahadur Shastri once travelled to his constituency in Allahabad where he addressed a public meeting in a village called Urva about 35 km from the city of Allahabad. In the course of his speech he uttered, for the first time, the famous slogan 'Jai Jawan Jai Kisan' and received unending applause from the people assembled there. He struck the right cord at the right time when we were fighting Pakistan on the border and at the same time battling the problem of food shortage in the country. I was a child and was present at the meeting in Urva. I am not sure whether saying the slogan 'Jai Jawan Jai Kisan' was an impromptu decision or was pre-intended. Whatever the reason, in no time this slogan resonated across the length and breadth of our country. And, it does resonate even today. Shastriji is closely identified with the slogan and vice versa. If it clicked, it was primarily because it is symbolic of India's dignity and honour.

Wisdom Window

Despite his humble demeanor Shastri was a man of honour. For him territorial integrity and self-reliance were most important. He knew that to preserve the territorial integrity of India it is important to motivate the soldier, and to get back self-reliance in food he needs to motivate the farmer to produce more. The slogan 'Jai Jawan Jai Kisan' was perhaps born from this well-considered thought.

It shows that Lal Bahadur Shastri was both strategic and creative.

War Heroes

(Circa 1965)

In the midst of the Indo-Pak war in 1965, Lal Bahadur Shastri wanted to visit the Military Hospital in Delhi to meet the injured soldiers. He asked me if I would like to come along and I said yes. It was around 11.30 in the morning that we reached the hospital. Shastriji was taken to different wards where he met jawans who had been injured while protecting the territorial integrity of our nation. As he moved further, he was taken to the ward where some officers were admitted. I could see that the army personnel were greatly motivated to meet their Prime Minister. Some of them even said that they forgot the pain of their wounds after seeing him.

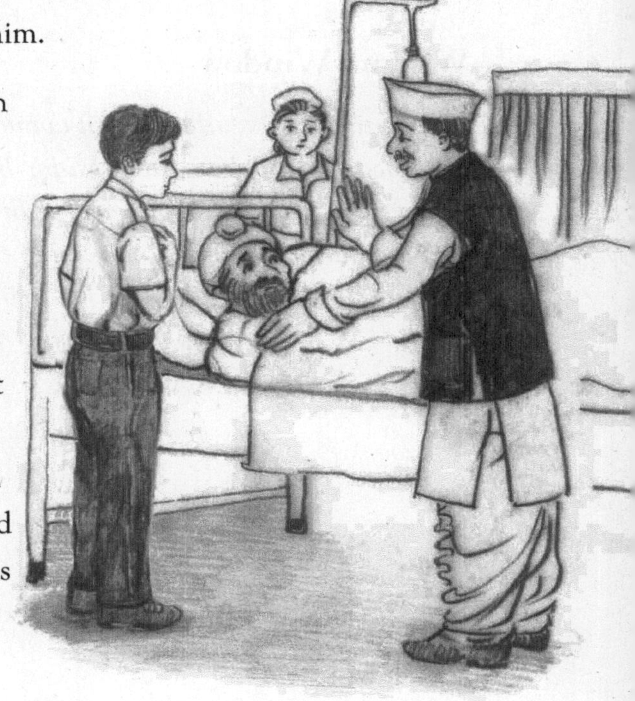

Shastriji was then taken to Major Bhupinder Singh who had been critically injured in a bomb blast. Since his body was burnt, it was covered with a white sheet. Shastriji went close to him and enquired about his condition. Major

Bhupinder Singh had tears in his eyes. Prime Minister Shastri said that he was a great soldier and still had many battles to fight. He would be alright soon and must cheer up. Major Bhupinder Singh said the tears in his eyes were not because of any physical pain but because of the fact that he could not stand up to salute his Prime Minister. Shastriji was greatly moved and I could see he was finding difficult to control his emotions.

Lal Bahadur Shastri gave the armed forces the opportunity to prove their might and they vindicated his expectations of them in full measure. The slogan 'Jai Jawan Jai Kisaan' is therefore a testimony to this and resonates across the length and breadth of India even today.

Wisdom Window

Patriotism is a sentiment that cannot be faked. Some people just live for the nation. Major Bhupinder Singh was in tears because of the immense pain he had to bear but despite that, he did not complain to the Prime Minister. Instead his deep respect for his Prime Minister came gushing forth.

True Hospitality

(Circa 1964)

Once Lal Bahadur had given appointment to some people from Bihar to come and meet him at his PM residence. By chance, on the same day a function in honour of a foreign dignitary also cropped up and it was imperative for Shastriji to attend that function. He got late at the function and the visitors from Bihar continued to wait for his arrival. After a long wait, the visitors decided to leave, utterly disappointed.

Shastriji came after they had left. The moment he came back from the function, the first thing he asked his Secretary was, "Where are the visitors from Bihar?" When the Secretary told him that they had just left after waiting for a long time, Shastriji got very disturbed. He asked his Secretary whether he knew where they had gone. On being told by him that they had to catch a bus from the bus-stop opposite PM residence, Shastriji instantly rushed towards the bus-stop. The Secretary was taken aback. He tried to prevent Shastriji saying, "What would people say if they came to know about it!" Shastriji retorted, "And what would the people say if they came to know that I did not meet the visitors after inviting them at my residence!"

The Secretary suggested that he himself would go and bring them back from the bus stop. Shastriji said, "No, I will have to go myself and beg for their pardon for this lapse. There

cannot be a better way than going myself." When he reached the bus-stop, he found them waiting for the bus. Shastriji expressed his deep regret and brought them back. One of the visitors said, "We saw so much in Delhi, but we would never forget that our Prime Minister is a symbol of true humility."

Wisdom Window

Shastri understood that to assuage the guests' hurt feelings, it would be right on his part to get them back from the bus stop himself rather than ask his secretary to do so, which he could have easily done. Shastri believed that the apology should be tendered by the person who has made the offence only then the apology heals.

Shastriji's visit to Amul, Anand

(Circa 1965)

This is a story of the White Revolution in India. Late Dr. V Kurien recollected that Lal Bahadur Shastri during his visit to Anand visited the Amul Dairy. Shastriji was the Prime Minister and he was greatly impressed with the efforts of Dr. Kurien. The Prime Minister at the end of his visit asked Dr. Kurien if he could establish many more Anands in the country. Dr. Kurien said he would love to do so and suggested to Shastriji to set up National Dairy Development Board (NDDB) for establishing and monitoring milk dairies across the country. His only condition was that the headquarters of NDDB should be in Anand and not in Delhi.

Prime Minister Shastri readily accepted the suggestion and told his Secretary on the spot that the headquarters of NDDB will be at Anand and not in Delhi. He also instructed that the Chairman of NDDB would be Dr. Kurien.

Dr. V Kurien said due to his astute foresight, India owed the White Revolution to Shri Lal Bahadur Shastri.

Wisdom Window

I feel the reasons why Shastri agreed to NDDB being headquartered in Anand were:

1. *He found Dr. Kurien to be a capable and professional worker and understood that having him at the helm of*

NDDB would ensure that the institution was run professionally.

2. *Shastri was not a patronage-driven person, and so it did not matter to him that he would have less control of NDDB since it was headquartered away from Delhi. In India, most of the institutes patronized by senior political leaders are either headquartered in their own state or in Delhi where these patronage driven leaders sit so this was quite a departure from typical power play.*

Super Communist

(Circa 1966)

After the 22 day war with Pakistan in September 1965, my father was upset as to why two neighbours fought with each other in a manner we did. He believed that every problem had a solution. A long term peace settlement with Pakistan was playing on his mind. Suddenly, there was a proposal from the Prime Minister of the Soviet Union, Mr. Alexei Kosygin, to host a meeting between the Indian Prime Minister, Shri Lal Bahadur Shastri, and the Pakistan President, General Ayub Khan. Initially, there were some reservations on the part of Shastriji but keeping in view the interests of both countries, he agreed to accept the invitation of Kosygin. Shastriji and Ayub Khan decided to meet in Tashkent, the capital of Uzbekistan (then Soviet Union), in the first week of January 1966.

Lal Bahadur Shastri left for Tashkent on January 3, 1966 hoping for a long term peace solution with Pakistan. Tashkent was very cold at that time of the year and Shastriji was carrying his usual khadi woollen coat. Prime Minister Kosygin realized that the coat that the Indian Prime Minister wore was not warm enough to ward off the snowy winter winds of Central Asia. Kosygin wanted to present a Russian overcoat to Shastriji but was not sure how to do so. Finally at a function, he presented a Russian coat as a gift to the Prime Minister hoping that he would wear it while in Tashkent. Next morning, Kosygin noticed that Shastriji was still wearing the khadi coat which he had brought from Delhi. Hesitatingly, he asked the Prime Minister whether he liked the overcoat which he gave to him. Shastriji replied in the affirmative and said, "It is really warm and very comfortable for me. However, I have lent it to one of my staff members who was not carrying a good woollen coat to wear in this severe winter. I will surely use your gift during my future trips to cold countries."

Prime Minister Kosygin narrated this incident during his welcome address at a cultural programme organized in honour of the Indian Prime Minister and the Pakistan President. Kosygin remarked, "We are communists but Prime Minister Shastri is a Super Communist."

Wisdom Window

Anil further recalls that during another visit to Soviet Union Shastri had been gifted a 20 carat gold watch which on his return he offered to Anil. Anil happily accepted it but wondered why his father wouldn't wear it. Shastri replied, "The leader of a poor nation cannot have flashy lifestyle."

Usually people look at people richer than them to compare what they do not possess. Shastri on the other hand always looked below him to see what others did not have and tried to fulfill their needs.

A Touching Tribute

(1966)

Shri Rajeshwar Prasad mentions about an incident when Shastriji's body was lying in State at 10, Janpath on the cruel night of 11th January 1966. Thousands of people were passing by the body of Shastriji silently and with tears. The guard at the gate had been instructed to see that everyone followed the queue but it was observed that people were breaking the queue and coming out of turn which was causing commotion and confusion.

The Security chief pulled up the guard for allowing people to come out of turn and break the line. His reply was, "Sir, what can I do? I keep begging them with folded hands not to break the queue, but they keep saying 'Who are you to stop me? Don't you know, I am so and so,' and, insist on going in then and there. But I am sure that the man who they have come to see would have listened to me and not broken the queue had he been alive."

Wisdom Window

Shastri was an icon of democracy and a keen advocate of equality. One facet of democracy is equal opportunity for all which is so well-reflected in the system of queuing up. A queue is a social equalizer.

Whether Shastri left any impact on us is a moot point but the guard who served him did realize that how different from rest of us was this Indian leader who he had had the good fortune to serve.

Select Bibliography

1) Adhikari, M., Lal Bahadur Shastri, Rajpal and sons, New Delhi, 1966
2) Manjula, Gudri Ka Lal, Lal Bahadur, UmeshPrakashan, New Delhi, 1966
3) Gupta, M.G., The Prime Minister of India, Agra,1989
4) Lajpat Rai, Young India, An interpretation and a History of the Nationalist Movement from within, Servants of the people society, Lahore, 1927
5) Baldoi, Ansuya Prasad, Karmyogi Lal Bahadur Shastri, Radha Publications, New Delhi, 1991
6) Prasad, Rajeshwar, Days with Lal Bahadur Shastri, Glimpses from the last Seven years, Allied Publishers Pvt. Ltd., New Delhi, 1991
7) Sharma, Ram, Lal Bahadur Shastri, An era of Transition in Indian foreign policy, Kaniska Publishers and Distributers, New Delhi, 2001
8) Hangen, Welles, After Nehru, Who?, Rupert Hart-Davis, London, 1963
9) Shri Lal Bahadur Shastri Sewa Niketan, Dharti Ka Lal, Lal Bahadur Shastri Smriti Granth, New Delhi, 1986
10) Shastri, Lal Bahadur, Selected Speeches of Lal Bahadur Shastri (11 June 1964 to 10 January 1966), Publications Division, Ministry of Information & Broadcasting, New Delhi, 1974